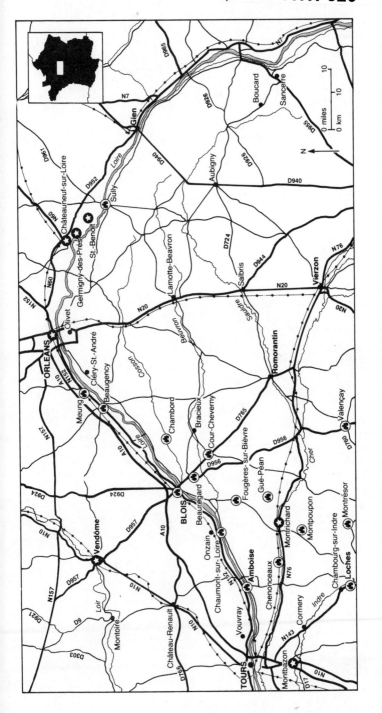

W9-ATH-326

FODOR'S

LOIRE
VALLEY

FODOR'S TRAVEL PUBLICATIONS, INC.
New York & London

ISBN 0-679-01381-4
ISBN 0-340-40065-X (Hodder & Stoughton edition)
First Edition

The following Fodor's guides are currently available; most are also published in a British edition by Hodder & Stoughton.

Country and Area Guides

Australia, New Zealand
& the South Pacific
Austria
Bahamas
Belgium & Luxembourg
Bermuda
Brazil
Canada
Canada's Maritime
Provinces
Caribbean
Central America
Eastern Europe
Egypt
Europe
France
Germany
Great Britain
Greece
Holland
Hungary
India, Nepal & Sri Lanka
Ireland
Israel
Italy
Japan
Jordan & the Holy Land
Kenya
Korea
Loire Valley
Mexico
New Zealand
North Africa
People's Republic
of China
Portugal
Province of Quebec
Scandinavia
Scotland
South America
South Pacific
Southeast Asia
Soviet Union
Spain
Sweden
Switzerland
Turkey
Yugoslavia

City Guides

Amsterdam
Beijing, Guangzhou,
Shanghai
Boston
Chicago
Dallas & Fort Worth
Florence & Venice
Greater Miami & the
Gold Coast
Hong Kong
Houston & Galveston
Lisbon
London
Los Angeles
Madrid
Mexico City &
Acapulco
Munich
New Orleans
New York City
Paris
Philadelphia
Rome
San Diego
San Francisco
Singapore
Stockholm, Copenhagen,
Oslo, Helsinki &
Reykjavik
Sydney
Tokyo
Toronto
Vienna
Washington, D.C.

U.S.A. Guides

Alaska
Arizona
Atlantic City & the
New Jersey Shore
California
Cape Cod
Chesapeake
Colorado
Far West
Florida
Hawaii
I–10: California to Florida
I–55: Chicago to
New Orleans
I–75: Michigan to Florida
I–80: San Francisco to
New York
I–95: Maine to Miami
New England
New Mexico
New York State
Pacific North Coast
South
Texas
U.S.A.
Virginia
Williamsburg, Jamestown
& Yorktown

Budget Travel

American Cities (30)
Britain
Canada
Caribbean
Europe
France
Germany
Hawaii
Italy
Japan
London
Mexico
Spain

Fun Guides

Acapulco
Bahamas
Las Vegas
London
Maui
Montreal
New Orleans
New York City
The Orlando Area
Paris
Puerto Rico
Rio
Riviera
St. Martin/Sint Maarten
San Francisco
Waikiki

Special-Interest Guides

The Bed & Breakfast Guide
Selected Hotels of Europe
Ski Resorts of North
America
Views to Dine by around
the World

MANUFACTURED IN THE UNITED STATES OF AMERICA
10 9 8 7 6 5 4 3 2 1

INTRODUCTION

The subject of this book is the château country of the Loire valley in France, an area that extends approximately from Orléans in the east to Angers in the west. It includes the lower valleys of a number of other rivers, the Cher, the Indre, the Vienne and the Loir (without an "e") chief among them. The Loire receives the waters of all these rivers and dominates the area.

The Loire is the longest river in France. It rises deep in the south of the country. While the Rhône is rolling down towards the Mediterranean, the little Loire, rising 5,000 feet up in the Cévennes, is flowing parallel to it but in the opposite direction. It continues northward for over half its length. Then, near Orléans, only 360 feet above sea level but with nearly half its length to go before it reaches the Atlantic at Nantes, it takes a wide bend westward. The stretch of about 150 miles from just above Orléans to just below Angers, together with places less than 30 miles from it, is our area, the Loire valley of centuries-old fame.

Sandbanks and Châteaux

The river has a changeable personality. If you come to the Loire in the spring you will see a noble river. At Rochefort-sur-Loire, our farthest point downstream, it will be carrying on average some 50,000 cubic feet of water per second. In August it will probably be down to 7,000 cubic feet. Upstream at Orléans, before its tributaries have joined it, it will be a mere trickle among the sandbanks.

But no one on or near the Loire has ever trusted to averages. Its fertile low-lying valley is subject to dramatic floods. For 1,000 years its population has been building and improving dykes. You will probably drive along the top of some of them. Perhaps, if it is high summer and the Loire has almost disappeared, you will wonder why they were made. But they are not a foot too high in flood years.

River transport on the Loire, though alternating floods and droughts, sandbanks and currents, made it a trying business, was important until the railways killed it. Indeed, the river has been described as the "greatest highway in France for 3,000 years or more.'' The boats went down with the current and up with the wind. There is no space to tell the fascinating story here, but those who are interested should make for the Musée de la Marine at Châteauneuf-sur-Loire.

But it is the châteaux of the Loire that constitute the region's chief claim to fame—the terms Loire and château are very nearly synonymous. There are, of course, châteaux dotted here and there all over France. But nowhere are they clustered as thickly as in the Loire. Why? There are several reasons. The presence of strategically sited and prosperous towns is one. The towns were there because of transport on the Loire. But the Loire was a barrier too, and proud towns grew up at bridge-heads. Fortresses—the first châteaux—were built by warlords to control certain key points, and for defense in troubled times.

There are other reasons, too. The valley was—and still is—richly productive land. The part between the Loire and the Cher has long been known as the garden of France. It is a pleasant place to live, with a kindly climate. In the lands above the valleys the weather is less kind, and the soil poorer. These lands are still forested. Warlords and kings hunted there, as presidents and visiting royalty still do. But as you head towards the north and the river, suddenly, as the land slopes down, you see vine-yards. In few other areas of France is *la douceur de la vie,* the sweetness of life, more alluring. Melons thrive, cattle grow sleek. Feudal lords grew rich; so did monks, building splendid abbeys and monasteries. It is a landscape made to the measure of man.

The early medieval Plantagenet kings, rulers of France and England, preferred to live here. Under the later medieval, Valois, kings, the Loire was in effect the capital of France. Châteaux—fortresses by now turning into palaces—sprang up at their command. They built them for their own use—the court was always on the move from one château to another—and as presents for favorites. Administrators who did well for them-selves and kept in favor also built lordly palaces and houses.

The material was often at hand. The Loire is blessed with an easily worked building stone, tufa, that hardens and whitens as it ages. Using this stone had a happy by-product too. Burrow into the limestone cliffs for your stone and you simultaneously tunnel out cool storage spaces for millions of bottles of local wine, or, should you be short of a vineyard, room to cultivate thousands of tons of mushrooms. Going a step further, you can also have two houses for the price of one: the carefully hol-lowed-out part of the cliff can provide living space. Even today, many such cave dwellings are still inhabited.

Around the year 1600 the power center shifted to Paris, but the châteaux and the tradition of luxurious living they stood for remained. Throughout the 17th and 18th centuries the great and the good continued buying or building. Even after the French Revolution, simple horny-handed millionaires and their aristocratic counterparts alike kept the realtors and stone masons of the Loire busy and affluent. Since the turn of the last century, such building has proved too expensive for even the wealthiest, while some of the bigger châteaux have gone beyond the means of individuals to maintain. But the age of tourism has now seen to it that these irreplaceable treasures have survived, with the State, local authorities and private bodies stepping in to run them, while the tourist helps foot the bill.

Seeing the Sights?

In four weeks' ruthless sightseeing, car-borne visitors can pay short visits to all the places we cover in this book. Record breakers can do it in less time. But they should not be complacent afterwards: our guide contains only a selection of what can be seen here. Some authorities say there are 400 châteaux in the Loire. Others talk of 1,000. It all depends what you mean by châteaux. It is easy to know when you have reached the top of a mountain, but hardly anyone can be said to have "done" the Loire valley. In any case, many things here should be seen several times, at different seasons. If you have only a short time to spare—assuming you can resist the (expensive) temptation to hire a helicopter and fly over all the main châteaux in one go—you could, for example, select a smallish area containing places that sound interesting and base yourself there, covering major and minor sights at your leisure and finding out from local tourist offices what happenings are due to take place, and going to them or staying well clear according to taste. This will leave pleasanter memories than three days spent largely on main roads in an effort to see St.-Benoit *and* Blois *and* Angers. For those happy few in a position to take a number of short vacations—people working temporarily in Paris, for example—the Loire valley is ideal: see it bit by bit.

It should be emphasized, however, that visiting the Loire does not have to mean visiting châteaux. There is a great deal more to do here besides sightsee. Indeed the French, who can sometimes take a notably carefree view of their heritage (though possibly not greatly different from the New Yorker who's never been up the Empire State Building or the Londoner who's never seen the Changing of the Guard), have vacationing here down to a comfortable art. Many do not go inside a single château. Of course, they will be aware of the châteaux. Some may even have seen some in the past. On a rainy day they might see another one, unless a glance at the local paper suggests a visit to a movie or some other town pleasure.

Rather, their concern here tends towards having a country vacation while taking full advantage of the urban facilities close at hand, and the good restaurants almost everywhere. Many of them hire *gîtes*—self-contained cottages. They like the country-side with its profusion of high-summer events and amusements. Concerts and music festivals, fairs, exhibits, sporting events, even a visit to a *son-et-lumière* in a château's grounds. And they take full advantage of the facilities for activities: horseback riding, fishing, canoeing, canal and river cruising (though not on the Loire itself, which is thought too difficult), windsurfing, waterskiing, rambling, cycling, and swimming on the many well-organized river beaches.

Weatherwise

The question on when to visit the Loire is easily answered: anytime, though naturally the summer is more pleasant than the winter. Winter here, December to the end of March, is temper-ately cold. The Loire freezes at Orléans only in exceptional years. Minor châteaux are closed, as are many of the more luxurious country hotels. April, May and June can be delightful. Everything is open, and there are not too many crowds. But some weekends in May can be busy, and hotels full. This is because of the number of one-day public holidays at this time of year inciting Parisians to leap into their cars and spend a long weekend in this accessible stretch of favored countryside. If one of these holidays falls on a Thursday or a Tuesday, the tempta-tion to make a very long weekend of it—what the French call making *un pont,* a bridge—can be irresistible.

In July and August it can sometimes be hot and humid. This is when the French take their vacations, as well as many other people, and there are large numbers of tourists seeing the sights and filling the hotels and restaurants, and blocking the roads. But the Loire never gets as crowded as the popular coastal resorts, especially the Riviera.

September and October—and parts of November in good years—can be even more delightful than the spring. All the French go back to work at the end of August, leaving plenty of room for everyone else. And if there are a few mists there is much in the way of mellow fruitfulness, especially in the vine-yards.

You can be unlucky and hit a rainy period, but the Loire has only 26 inches of rain a year, evenly distributed throughout the year. To encounter persistently bad weather you would have to be unlucky indeed.

LOIRE BRIEFING

Finding Out

Make the French National Tourist Office the first stop on your visit to the Loire. They have offices throughout the globe and can supply a wealth of information on France, much of it free and all of it useful. Their principal offices are:

- **In the U.S.:** 610 Fifth Ave., New York, NY 10020 (212–757–1125); 645 North Michigan Ave., Chicago, IL 60611 (312–337–6301); 103 World Trade Center, Dallas, TX 75258 (214–742–7011); 9401 Wilshire Blvd., Suite 314, Beverly Hills, CA 90212 (213–272–2661).
- **In Canada:** 1981 Ave. McGill College, Montreal, Quebec H3A 2W9 (514–931–3855); 1 Dundas St. West, Suite 2405, Box 8, Toronto, Ontario M5G 1Z3 (416–593–4717).
- **In the U.K.:** 178 Piccadilly, London W.1 (01–491–7622).

Within France, tourist offices fall into two categories: the central departmental offices that coordinate tourist information for each of the administrative *départements* which France is divided into (see below); and local tourist offices. Most of the information they distribute is in English or devised to be easily understood by those with no French. But in the larger tourist offices there is always someone who speaks English. When arriving anywhere it is sensible to make first for the tourist office, if only to pick up a town plan (*un plan*). It will be called *Office de Tourisme* or, in smaller places, *Syndicat d'Initiative*. All display the international "**i**" sign, meaning "information."

The principal departmental offices in the Loire are: **Maine-et-Loire,** BP 852, 49008 Angers (tel. 41–88–23–85); **Indre-et-Loire,** 16 rue de Buffon, 37032 Tours (tel. 47–61–61–23); **Loir-et-Cher,** 11 pl. du Château, 41000 Blois (tel. 54–78–55–50); **Loiret,** 3 rue de la Bretonnerie, 45000 Orléans (tel. 38–66–24–10).

For written enquiries only, there are two other useful offices that publish and distribute information of a precise nature. These are the "regional" offices that oversee the individual *départements.* The Loire includes two of these: Centre, covering Indre-et-Loire, Loir-et-Cher, and Loiret; and Pays de la Loire, covering Maine-et-Loire. Their addresses are: **Centre**—Comité Régional de Tourisme, 10 rue du Colombier, 45023 Orléans, Cedex; **Pays de la Loire**—Comité Régional de Tourisme, 3 pl.

St.-Pierre, 44000 Nantes.

The addresses of local tourist offices are given in the "Fast Facts" at the end of each gazetteer entry.

Tours to the Loire

The Loire valley is the subject of numerous tours, some familiar in style and content, others a bit more exotic. Along familiar lines, several of the major tour operators offer a stop in the Loire as a part of their larger sampling of the French country and culture. Globus Gateway spends three days in the Loire valley as part of its 12-day "Windmills, Vineyards and Châteaux" tour. Included are visits to Orléans, Blois, and two châteaux, Chenonceau and Amboise. Cost is $748–778, depending on the season; airfare is not included. Maupintour offers something similar as part of its 12-day "France Highlights" program. As Maupintour's accommodations are somewhat fancier, the cost is somewhat higher: $1,598–1,748, with the same seasonal and airfare considerations. Travcoa's two tours in the area, "Normandy, Brittany and Châteaux" (13 days, $2,495); and "Exotic France" ($3,795 for 19 days, $6,295 for 30), emphasize small groups (20 or less), and feature wine-tasting expeditions, stops at Orléans, Cheverny, Chambord, and similar spots, and offer, as a highlight, a dinner party as the guest of a countess at a château in the region.

Moving toward the more exotic, one might consider barging or ballooning—or indeed barging *and* ballooning—one's way across the valley. Continental Waterways and Horizon Cruises Ltd. both offer trips on luxurious barges that travel the canals and rivers that crisscross the Loire valley and nearby Burgundy. Both also offer the chance to float above it all in a hot-air balloon.

Barges aren't a form of mass transport; most have room for 20 or less. The trips tend to be four or seven days' long, and emphasize food and drink, both on the barge, where meals are large and sumptuous, and on land, where wine and cheese tasting expeditions are common. Continental Waterways sends its barge, the *Escargot,* on seven-day cruises down the Loire, though generally farther upstream than the château country, with stops at Sancerre, Charité-sur-Loire, Cuffy, Nevers, Château d'Aprement, and Decize, among others. Bouts of tennis, aerobics, and land-leave shopping trips are all available if desired. And a hot-air balloon trip may be tagged on, to see from above where one was floating below. Cost is $1,140–

1,540, depending on the season. Again, airfare isn't included. The barge trips offered by Horizon Cruises are similar, although a somewhat more extensive ballooning option is available. Four- and seven-day balloon trips are offered, as trips in their own right, or as extensions of barge cruises. Note that on a balloon trip, the actual travel is by bus; balloon sightseeing trips are offered each evening before dinner. Horizon Cruises' barge trips run $1,500–2,500 for a week, with the usual considerations. Ballooning runs $1,800 for four days, $3,000 for seven.

For those who find ballooning too sedate, Horizon Cruises offers a three-day/two-night helicopter tour, with stops at Chambord, Cheverny, Chenonceau, Boucard and Jussy-Champagne. Cost? $2,995.

Then there are those who would prefer to stay land-bound. For those who aren't thrilled by ballooning, but would still like an unusual way to see the region, Claremont Riding Holidays offers an 11-day exploration of the region on horseback, called "Châteaux of the Loire." Tours begin in Blois or Tours. Accommodations, meals, horses, guides, and baggage transportation are all included. Accommodations are in private châteaux, or château hotels. Tours are run from June to October, and cost $1,478.

Also available are cycling tours, from Country Cycling Tours, two-week excursions that stop in Beaugency, Chambord, Chinon, Saumur, and other spots in the area. Guides are included, as well as a van to carry baggage and weary cyclists. Tours are launched May–October, and cost $1,495.

Finally, if you're a do-it-yourselfer, Auto Venture will help you plan an itinerary, make auto and hotel reservations, and send you off to discover the Loire on your own.

Tour Operators. *American Express,* 822 Lexington Ave., New York, NY 10021 (212–758–6510); 12 Richmond St. East, Toronto, Ont. M5C 1M5 (416–868–1044).

Auto Venture, 920 Logan Bldg., Seattle, WA 98101 (800–426–7502).

Cityrama, 347 Fifth Ave., New York, NY 10016 (212–683–8120).

Claremont Riding Stables, 175 West 89th St., New York, NY 10024 (212–724–5101).

Continental Waterways, 11 Beacon St., Boston, MA (800–227–1281).

Country Cycling Tours, 140 West 83rd St., New York, NY 10024 (212–874–5151).

Globus Gateway, 95–25 Queens Blvd., Rego Park, NY 11374 (718–268–1700).

Horizon Cruises, Ltd., c/o Hemphill Harris, 16000 Ventura Blvd., Ste. 200, Encino, CA 91436 (818–906–8086).

Maupintour, 1515 St. Andrew's Dr., Lawrence, KS 66044 (913–843–1211).

Mountain Travel, 1398 Solano Ave., Albany, CA 94706 (800–227–2384).

Salt and Pepper Tours, 7 West 36th St., Ste. 1500, New York, NY 10018 (212–736–8226).

Travcoa, 875 North Michigan Ave., Chicago, IL 60611 (312–951–2900).

Travel Concepts, Inc., 373 Commonwealth Ave., Boston, MA 02115 (617–266–8450).

Voyage International, 12029 Buftleton St., Philadelphia, PA 19116 (215–677–7104).

Getting There

The Loire is nothing if not an accessible region, easy to reach and easy to travel around in. Coming from either the U.S. or the U.K., the options available to you are considerable, whether you plan to travel on your own or take a tour, either fully or partly escorted. The alternatives can indeed seem very nearly endless. Certainly they are sufficiently numerous to make it impossible in so short a book to list them all here. It is sufficient to say that any good travel agent or branch of the French National Tourist Office should be able to give you the alternatives. All we have attempted is to sketch out the bare bones of the travel possibilities.

● **By Air:** You can't actually fly to the Loire itself from the States—Tours and Nantes on the Atlantic coast both have airports but no intercontinental flights—but there are frequent and regular flights to Paris from most major departure points in the U.S., Los Angeles and New York in particular. Air, rail and road connections from Paris to the Loire are excellent; see below for details. Air France has flights to Nantes in the summer from London (Heathrow), but again it is generally easier to fly to Paris from the U.K. and continue from there.

● **By Train:** Train and ferry connections from the U.K. to the Loire are plentiful. There are two routes from the U.K., one via Dover and Calais or Boulogne and then through Paris, the other via Portsmouth and Caen or St.-Malo on the overnight ferry. Both routes have excellent rail connections to the Loire, but if you have heavy bags the former, with its easier rail/ship/rail interchanges, is simplest.

● **By Car:** Going by car from the U.K. the choice of route is great. Nearly all the Channel crossings are suitable. It really depends where you're starting from and how quickly you want to get there. Most of the main centers can be reached comfortably in one day from London, say, using the Dover–Calais/Boulogne crossings and then zooming down the A1 highway to Paris and round the *boulevard périphérique* to the A10 to Orléans and Tours. Alternatively, you can drive more slowly and scenically across Normandy and then down into the Loire. The roads from the more westerly Channel ports—Dieppe, Le Havre, Caen, Cherbourg and Roscoff—are not rapid, though very pretty, but the ferry crossings to them are longer.

All the ferry companies offer a wide range of touring holidays around the Loire, either on fixed routes with pre-booked accommodations or a go-as-you-please basis. By and large they are excellent value for money. Details from travel agents.

Getting Around

● **By Train:** The Loire has an excellent local rail network, indeed almost the only stumbling block is coming to terms with the idiosyncratic timetabling. This minor inconvenience aside, it's amazing just how much you can do, so long as you try not to cram in too much. The principal rail line follows the Loire itself from Orléans in the east to Nantes in the west, passing through Blois, Tours, Saumur and Angers. This naturally means that places away from the river can't be visited by train, but a good network of local buses helps fill in most of the gaps. Indeed there are very few places that can't be visited either by train or bus or some combination of the two. A number of these buses are run by the railways, others by local companies. Those which connect with trains are detailed in the back of the rail timetable. For further information, *see* "By Bus" below.

If you plan to visit the Loire for a week or more and intend to do a great deal of traveling by train then it might be worth while buying a "France Vacances" rail pass, to purchase a go-anywhere rail ticket giving unlimited travel for a specific period. But it's not really designed for use in a single area such as the Loire, and you will have to travel almost non-stop to get your money's worth. Similarly, if you're visiting the Loire as part of a longer European trip, a Eurailpass—similar to the France Vacances ticket but good for the whole of Europe except the U.K.—is worth considering. Both must be bought *before* you leave home. Otherwise, buy your tickets as you go along: French rail fares are pleasantly low. There are also some useful fare deals. If you're married (or just living together; the French aren't very particular about these things) get a "Carte Couple." This entitles one of a traveling pair to half-price travel on all non-rush hour trains. Women over 60 and men over 62 qualify for a "Carte Vermeil"; this also gives half-price on all off-peak trains.

● **By Car:** Most visitors to the Loire use a car, and for good reasons. This is undoubtedly the best way to see the area, with nowhere inaccessible, short distances, and a choice of minor and major roads for slow or swift traveling as mood or circumstance dictate. The road network is sufficiently dense—though a good map is essential to get the best out of it—to permit you to take minor ones when going to see major châteaux, taking in lesser châteaux en route and other things of interest lurking in the green and smiling countryside. But even for those who prefer little roads with flowers in the hedges and cows looking over the gates, the A10 highway is of strategic importance. As we say, it runs from Paris to Orléans, and on to Tours, with exits at Meung, Blois and Amboise on the way: a dull but quick way of linking up the interesting districts east of Tours. After Tours it leaves the Loire and heads south towards Bordeaux. The result is that the ordinary main roads along the Loire west of Tours, towards Saumur and Angers, are more traffic laden than those east of Tours, which are duplicated by the A10.

Car hire is easy to arrange in all the larger towns. We give addresses of leading car-hire companies in the "Fast Facts" of those towns with them. French railways operate a useful service: a self-drive car can await you at the rail stations of Orléans, Blois, Tours or Angers, and you can drop it off at any of those stations, or at any of a vast number of other stations in France, including those in Paris.

● **By Bus:** Local services are fairly good, and a handy supplement to train routes. But the major problem for the tourist is finding out what's available. Major services—as well as those that link with trains—are listed in the back of the rail timetable. Otherwise, the best bet is to ask at the local tourist office, either in advance or on the spot. As a general rule, the more rural routes will have only a few buses a day, usually in the early morning and late afternoon. In main towns buses leave from the Gare Routière, often close to the rail station. In smaller towns and villages ask for the "ârret des cars"; it will normally be centrally located.

In addition to regular bus routes, there are a host of bus trips, either whole or half day, from all the larger tourist centers. Details from local tourist offices.

● **By Bicycle:** The bicycle is worth serious consideration by those who spurn cars. The Loire is an ideal region for cycling, with few hills to speak of and delightful countryside to ride through. Moreover, many of the most interesting places are within an hour's gentle pedaling of one another. In fact, so tempting are the possibilities for a bicycle holiday here that a good many flexible vacation packages have sprung up. Probably the most convenient is French railroad's bicycle hire service, where bikes can be hired at Tours, Langeais, Amboise, Chinon, Loches, Onzain and Blois railroad stations in the Loire (and about 250 elsewhere in France) by the day or longer and left at any other main rail station. Advance reservations are advisable in the high season though. You can also take bikes on a number of French trains, but not all, so check beforehand. There are also a number of fly/cycle and drive/cycle package vacations. For the not so energetic, your luggage will be sent on ahead of you every day. For the more *sportif,* your pared-down equipment is packed onto the bike and more arduous routes chosen. Details from travel agents and French National Tourist Offices.

Where to Stay

Finding a hotel in the Loire is not a difficult business. At the top end of the scale there are a number of magnificent five-star establishments such as the celebrated Château d'Artigny at Montbazon. At the lower end of the range there are any number of small family-run country hotels offering simple but reliable comforts, very often with surprisingly good restaurants to boot. Indeed many people find that the best way to explore the Loire, at any rate with a car, is to use exactly this type of hotel, picking your way from place to place by pleasant minor roads, making only occasional daytime visits to larger towns. In between, there are modestly comfortable hotels everywhere—in towns, villages, or all by themselves in a country garden—offering two- and three-star facilities.

Most good hotels, at all levels, are independently owned and run, though some belong to, or are affiliated to, a number of hotel groups and chains. Novotel and Ibis are two such. Then there are also a number of loose groupings of hotels. These are not centrally directed but get together to centralize their publicity. Among the most interesting are those whose hotels are actually châteaux themselves. The most famous—and expensive—is the Relais et Châteaux group. Those belonging to another group—Châteaux-Hôtels Indépendents—are mostly less expensive. Two smaller groups are Château Accueil and La Castellerie. At the cheapest end of the scale there is the Logis de France group. These are simple one- and two-star places, found in villages rather than towns. Lists of all these groups and associations are available free from the French National Tourist Offices in the States and the U.K.

You can place a fair amount of reliance on these groups. The French are keen grumblers when a hotel fails to give satisfaction, and have no hesitation in writing to complain to the group's headquarters. Unsatisfactory hotels find themselves dropped from the group.

Our listings contain only a small fraction of the Loire's hotels, selected from over the whole price range. Local tourist offices have lists of all hotels in their areas with current prices.

Hotel Prices and Grades: We have divided the hotels in our listings into three simple price grades: Expensive, indicated by (E) after the hotel's name; Moderate, indicated by (M); and Inexpensive, indicated by (I). These grades are determined solely by price.

Two people in a double room can expect to pay around 450 fr. and up in an Expensive hotel; 300 to 450 fr. in a Moderate hotel; and 100 to 300 fr. in an Inexpensive hotel.

It must be emphasized, however, that prices can vary enormously within each category and, confusingly, sometimes within an individual hotel. One establishment may well have a couple of special rooms costing considerably more than the others, and/or some costing considerably less. Check very carefully the cost of your room when you make your reservations. And check the price posted up in your room. Make sure it's the same as that you agreed.

● **Self-catering:** There is much to be said in favor of catering for oneself. There is camping, of course, and the Loire valley abounds in camp sites. These are officially graded, from one to four stars. The latter have such things as heated swimming pools, restaurants, children's playgrounds, and cost as much as a simple hotel. At the other end of the scale, closer to nature, there is *camping à la ferme,* where a farmer offers simple facilities to a few campers.

Alternatively, you can hire a cottage or a self-contained part of a house in the country. This is easily done through the Gîtes de France organization. These Gîtes, as they are known, or Gîtes Ruraux, have all the basic facilities—proper toilet, bath or shower, cooking equipment, etc.—everything in fact but sheets and towels, though these can usually be hired for a small extra cost. All are inspected and graded (from one to three ears of corn) by the Fédération Nationale des Gîtes de France. Descriptive lists of Gîtes in every *département* or region can be had by writing to main tourist offices, including overseas branches of the French National Tourist Office. Gîtes tend to be fully booked for July and August by the French, who are fond of passing their long vacations in this way, but outside those months there is usually no difficulty in finding one if the operation is started a couple of months in advance.

Apartments in towns like Tours, Blois or even Amboise do not come under the Gîtes de France umbrella. There, the local tourist office will provide lists of agents who deal with such things.

Eating and Drinking

As for eating, tourists have few problems. Even the snack bars and fake-looking eating places near the entrances to major châteaux and other tourist hotspots, there to make a fast franc in the high season and shunned by Frenchmen with traditional standards in the matter of gastronomy, are better than one might expect from experiences in some other countries. And for tourists who do not much care what they eat, *le fast-food* (hamburger joints, pizzerias, and *crêperies* —pancake houses) has made its appearance. The young French quite like it, much to the disgust of their elders.

Proper restaurants for proper French food served at proper French times—about 12:30 and 8 P.M.—abound. An effort is made in some books to describe Loire gastronomy, but in fact Loire food is simply French food at its best, or nearly so. The region has everything: cattle, poultry, game in season, fish from river and sea, butter, cream, wine . . . and excellent fruit and vegetables: the "garden of France" is a vegetable garden, sending its products to the best tables in Paris, but fortunately keeping plenty for local use. The Loire will be able to meet any gourmet's expectations.

The great temples of gastronomy may be in Paris and Lyons, but the Loire boasts a number of excellent expensive restaurants. None of the top 20 restaurants of France is here—the ones found in glossy magazines the world over—but there are some in the next hundred and plenty in the next thousand, offering delight at a reasonable price. It is doubtful if in any other region of France—and scarcely conceivable if in any other country—one can so confidently rely on eating so well at any restaurant chosen at random, provided only that it seems to be patronized by locals. That remark applies not only to the expensive place where specimens of *la nouvelle cuisine* appear on vast octagonal plates, but also to the inexpensive restaurant where the tablecloth is made of paper and you might be expected to use the same knife and fork for two courses.

Our assertion that there are no real gastronomic specialties in the Loire valley would be hotly disputed by local enthusiasts. And indeed a keen Loire inhabitant will find differences between the food of Beaugency and Angers. We are looking at the matter from the point of view of a New Yorker or a Londoner. However, when it comes to doing the marketing for an easily prepared meal in a gîte or for a picnic, we must sing the praises of the Loire's *charcuteries*. These can be roughly translated as delicatessens, or cooked-meat shops, or pork butchers' shops. They are particularly good in the Loire. Two local specialties among the many items on sale are *rillettes* and *rillons*. The former is a kind of meat paste, and the latter long-cooked lumps of pork. Neither sounds exciting, put like that, but enthusiasm comes with tasting specimens from a good *charcuterie*.

Loire wines can be very good. Enthusiasts should call at tourist offices and Maisons du Vin for advice and leaflets on visiting the vineyards of Vouvray, Saumur, Chinon and other places where the wines of Anjou and Touraine are made. These are mostly white, but there are some good reds in the Chinon-Bourgueil district. They cannot rival the very best wines from Bordeaux or Burgundy, which nowadays cost a fortune, but the better ones occupy an honorable place near the top, while the inexpensive ones give honest pleasure.

Restaurant Prices and Grades: As with hotels, we have divided the restaurants in our listings into three simple grades: Expensive, indicated by (E) after the restaurant's name; Moderate, indicated by (M); and Inexpensive, indicated by (I). These grades are determined solely by price.

Per person, excluding wine, you can expect to pay around 150 fr. and up in an Expensive restaurant; 80 to 150 fr. in a Moderate restaurant; and 40 to 80 fr. in an Inexpensive restaurant.

It can't be stressed too strongly, however, that the price of a meal in France varies vastly according to whether you order *à la carte* or from the fixed-price menu, *le menu* as it is called. The former, although offering more choice, is invariably *much* the more expensive for a meal with the same number of courses as *le menu*. Not all restaurants have a *menu* of course, but if they do it's always worth choosing it if you want maximum nourishment for minimum outlay.

Visiting Châteaux

The Loire tourist need not be a historian or an expert in architecture, though if he has absolutely no interest in either of those matters he might be happier somewhere else—in the nightclubs of Paris, the solitude of the mountains or on a smart beach somewhere. But equally, it is possible to enjoy yourself in the Loire—fishing, eating and pottering by car, on a bicycle or on foot—without seeing a single château or knowing Joan of Arc from Catherine de Médicis. But châteaux is what the Loire is about for most people, and there will be a lot of them in this book.

The Loire valley has long been a land of what is now called tourism. Originally, it was a leisured and aristocratic affair. One was invited to châteaux, or rented a house and hired servants to supplement those one had brought. Then in the mid-1900s the railways came. Tourists took advantage of the fact that developing commerce had implanted inns, big and small, in the towns and villages. But railway tourists could not always see the châteaux. Either they were abandoned and in a more or less ruinous and unsafe condition, or they were lived in. In the latter case, if the family was away in Paris, a caretaker might show you round in exchange for a tip. But the State and the town councils were already beginning to take over, repair, furnish and maintain many of the abandoned châteaux, preserving the country's cultural heritage and developing the tourist industry at the same time. As for the privately-owned châteaux, there are some wealthy people who can still afford to keep strangers out, with a big "Château Privé" notice at the park gates. But more usually the ancestral château is kept under repair by admission charges, with the family living in one wing.

But whether the château is state owned, owned by some public body or privately owned, the tourist has to keep putting his hand into his pocket. His château visiting is not going to be paid for by the French taxpayer, though it may be subsidized. But prices are not high. Think of a visit to a château as costing about half the price of a movie theater seat and you won't be far wrong.

We specify in each château listing in our gazetteer whether you can wander around freely or are shepherded from room to room by a guide, with doors unlocked and relocked as you come and go. The latter system can cause some irritation, especially if the guide speaks only French. If this is the case, there are usually leaflets in English which you can buy or borrow. There are normally English-speaking guides at the major châteaux in high season, but you may have to wait for a suitable group to assemble. Similarly, if we say that a guided visit takes 45 minutes, for example, arrive at least an hour before closing time. Other drawbacks: the worst is that one must expect to be hurried through some rooms where one might wish to linger, and to be kept too long in other rooms while the story of some royal favorite is trotted out for the umpteenth time. It is also virtually impossible to leave a guided tour in midstream.

But whether French- or English-speaking, there are good guides and bad guides, enthusiastic and articulate guides and perfunctory guides who recite a spiel they have learnt by heart. In both cases, most of them would like a tip at the end of the visit, and will place themselves conveniently to receive their tribute. If you reward those who you feel have done a good job with a tip of between a quarter and a half of the admission charge, and refrain from tipping the others, it can do nothing but good.

But let us not grumble if we are sometimes herded around instead of wandering at our own sweet whim. Unguided visits are possible only when there is nothing that could be stolen or vandalized, or where the château is so popular that the admission fees are enough to pay for an attendant in every room. One's time in the Loire would be the poorer if those were the only châteaux one could see.

Finally, it is vital to say a few words about the vexed question of château opening times. These can, frankly, be a nightmare, varying enormously and very often for no reason discernible to man. Though we give opening times for all the châteaux we list, double check them wherever you can with the local tourist office. It's a question of being safe and avoiding making that special trip only to find a locked door because it's the director's mother-in-law's birthday.

Nonetheless, there are certain general points that can be made reasonably confidently. The first is that the larger and the most popular châteaux tend to have the most regular opening times, though most of them will still probably close for one day a week and over lunch, except, in some cases, in July and August. The second point is that summer and winter opening times are not at all the same thing. Even the biggest châteaux will have restricted opening times in the winter, while many of the smaller ones may well not be open at all, especially if they're privately owned. So, as we say, double check wherever you can.

Some French Words

This list is not intended as a general vocabulary for the tourist in France. Rather, it is simply a list of potentially misleading words that crop up frequently in the Loire, plus a few general terms for which there is no satisfactory English translation.

—*Cave.* Not a cave (which is *une grotte*) but a place where wine is stored. Wine-makers want you to stop at their *caves* to sample their wine and buy some.

—*Château.* This covers a multitude of buildings: a warlike stronghold (though that should properly be called a *château fort*), a palace, or a medium-sized or big country house built any time in the last 1,000 years, even yesterday. But if it is a lordly mansion in a town it is *un hôtel.*

—*Chemin de ronde.* A walkway behind the battlements at the top of a fortified wall or tower.

—*Dégustation.* Tasting, or indeed consuming, usually of wine. *Dégustation gratuite* means free tasting.

—*Donjon.* A fortified tower or keep. It is often mistranslated in tourist leaflets as dungeon, the French word for which is *un cachot.*

—*Gîte.* A cottage or self-contained part of a house used for a short-term vacation rental.

—*Gothique.* Unlike *roman* (see below), this means what it seems to, i.e. Gothic, both the period and the architectural style of that period, generally characterized by pointed, rather than rounded, arches and, in churches, a tall, skeletal stone frame with large windows supported by flying buttresses.

—*Hôtel.* A large building in a town, often a hotel in the English sense but not always so. *Hôtel de ville* means town hall, and *Hôtel des Postes* means main post office. The private houses of a wealthy man were his *hôtel* in town and his *château* in the country.

—*Machicoulis.* Machicolations; that is, openings at floor level in a castle in projecting parts at the top of walls or towers, through which nasty things can be dropped or poured on attackers below.

—*Montgolfière.* A hot-air balloon: the name comes from the Montgolfier brothers, who invented the hot-air balloon in the 18th century. In the Loire they are used for taking tourists for expensive flights over châteaux.

—*Place.* A square in a town, whether rectangular, circular, or any other shape.

—*Roman.* Not Roman (as in Roman Empire), which is *romain* in French, but Romanesque, an architectural term for the massive style with rounded arches that preceded the Gothic (and is sometimes also inaccurately called Norman). Beware of mistranslations in tourist leaflets: there are practically no Roman buildings in the Loire, but plenty which are *roman*.

—*Son-et-lumière.* Literally, sound and light. These are open-air shows given at châteaux mainly on summer nights, usually providing an historical pageant.

—*Troglodytique.* Literally, troglodytic, or living in caves. But this is misleading if you think of cave men. In many places along the Loire the soft white limestone cliffs have been carved into proper houses with proper fronts (doors and windows, and so on), and with chimneys projecting up into the fields above.

PERSPECTIVES

A visit to the Loire inevitably means coming to grips with the history of the region—and sometimes of France too—and its architecture. Visit almost any château or historic town and you will be faced with tales of Catherine de Médicis, François I, Foulques Nerra, Gregory of Tours, and a whole host of other fascinating but frequently confusing French men and women. Likewise, explanations of Gothic and Romanesque arches, flying buttresses, bosses, crenellations, Vetruvian openings, and other architectural terms in châteaux and churches can also confuse rather than enlighten. So here we have devised two simple aides-mémoire to the history and architecture of the Loire that should sort out some of the salient points.

Architecture in the Loire

The Loire valley can be enjoyed without seeing a single château. And châteaux can be enjoyed without knowing a thing about architecture (or the tremendous engineering problems of spanning great areas with stone only and no steel beams or reinforced concrete). But for interested beginners we attempt, in the following four pages, to distinguish the four main types of building found in the Loire's châteaux.

1—The medieval fortress

Angers
Chinon
Loches (part only)
Plessis-Bourré
Sully

2—The Renaissance fortress

Beaugency (château Dunois)
Fougères-sur-Bièvre
Langeais
Loches (part only)
Montreuil-Bellay
Montsoreau
Saumur
Ussé

3—The Renaissance château

Amboise
Azay-le-Rideau
Chambord
Chaumont
Chenonceau
Gué-Péan
Le Lude
Montrésor
Villandry

4—The Classical château

Beauregard
Cheverny
Montgeoffroy
Valençay

Angers

Angers—the medieval fortress

The château at Angers is a functional building, designed to withstand sudden raids, revolts and long sieges. It was started by Foulques Nerra around 1000. Imagine the 17 towers and the massive curtain walls as they were in the days of Louis IX. He reconstructed and improved Angers between 1228 and 1238: each tower was one or two stories higher, with pointed roofs and external wooden *chemins de ronde* with machicolations.

Attackers could try to get across the moat while the defenders shot at them with arrows and cross-bow bolts from the slit windows. If successful, they would then have to use scaling ladders to climb the walls, or bring up cumbersome wooden towers. Or they could use battering rams to breach the walls. Or try to batter down the portcullis and door; but notice how vulnerable attackers are, outside the doorway, and consider their problems as they file into the keep. Alternatively, if they bored a long tunnel—awkward with that moat—they could excavate a cavern, using timber props, and set fire to the props in the hope that the wall would collapse. But the most practical solution was always treachery or starvation.

Saumur

Saumur—the Renaissance fortress

Fortresses like Angers were meant to look grim, advertising horrid problems for attackers and unpleasant conditions for prisoners in the dungeons. With Saumur, a touch of elegance has arrived. It is a thoroughly practical castle, of course: look at the tower, with its battlements, the *chemin de ronde* behind them and the machicolations, and the well-defended gate-house. Certainly it could have withstood a siege. But the style suggests a decorative impulse too. Saumur was built in the second half of the 14th century, around 1370. The famous illustration of it in the *Très Riches Heures* of the duc de Berry, painted around 1400, shows a riot of high pointed roofs and pinnacles—though these were modified in later centuries—while in the 16th century the outer fortifications were built (as a defense against cannon). But decent size windows have re-placed slits. It is not romantically foolish to think of love-sick princesses leaning out of these windows, and of chivalric tour-naments, with all the trappings of cloth-of-gold, and banquets with trumpeters. The time has not yet arrived when every rich noble will insist on a decorative drawbridge and defensive tower or two to impress the neighbors. But one can feel it coming.

Azay-le-Rideau

Azay-le-Rideau—the Renaissance château

Now what has happened? It's the Renaissance, brought to France by Charles VIII at the end of the 15th century. Soon afterwards François I's treasurer, Gilles Berthelot, entrusted the building of a château to his wife. This was not to be a higgledy-piggledy concatenation of bits and pieces, however big and strong, but a planned whole. It was Azay-le-Rideau.

It still looks Gothic from a distance, with its towers and moat. But the moat is the river Indre, and its purpose is to provide a pleasing reflection, adding a further symmetry to this jewel of architecture. Balance, harmony, and grace. The machicolations have turned into an agreeable decorative feature. Above them, the *chemin de ronde* and the battlements have become part of the living space—gracious living indeed. Those big windows let in light from the sky, and light reflected from the waters below. Inside, it is no surprise to find a wide straight staircase with landings, instead of the awkward spiral staircases of earlier châteaux. Those were useful for defense, but this was very far from Madame Berthelot's concern. She wanted a nice looking house in a nice looking garden, with nice big rooms and nice big windows—and convenient staircases for sweeping skirts.

Cheverney

Cheverny—the Classical château

There's no suggestion of a fortress here, whether grimly practical or daintily romantic. Cheverny is an example of the Classical style in its perfection, built between 1604 and 1634.

The drawing shows some characteristic details of this style: the window architraves; the balance of the vertical lines and the horizontal; the interesting but disciplined variations in the treatment of the dormer windows; part of the rather fanciful roof design. But the essential feature of the Classical château's design is symmetry. Cheverny stands, gleaming white under its slate-blue roofs, in exact symmetrical dignity. As you walk up the straight drive to the front door you fully expect to see "My Lord advancing with majestic mien/Smit with the mighty pleasure, to be seen." Englishman Alexander Pope, author of these lines, did not care for this sort of architecture; he preferred something much more cunningly "natural."

If today this style seems boring, it is perhaps the fault of architects at the turn of the century who built banks, hotels and even railway stations with steel frames and then stuck fake "respectable" facades on them, with "Classical" bits and pieces. A visit to Cheverny day can be a stimulating corrective.

Loire History

Some Useful Dates in the Loire and Elsewhere

1st century A.D. onwards. The Roman Empire includes most of France (Gaul). Important Roman towns in the Loire valley include Tours, where parts of the Roman city wall are still visible.

371 St.-Martin, ex-soldier in the Roman army, becomes bishop of Tours.

476 The Romans leave France.

481 Clovis king of the Franks.

594 Death of Gregory, bishop of Tours, and author of best-selling *History of the Franks*.

800 onwards. Troublesome Scandinavians sacking and looting in the Loire valley and elsewhere in France. In England they are called Vikings.

911 A number of these Scandinavians settle in France, and become Christians. They are called Normans, or "north" men, and are based in Normandy.

972–1040 Life of Foulques Nerra ("Black Fulk"), count of Anjou. He is a Touraine warlord and spends his life fighting, plundering and murdering (and making good by going on three Crusades—where of course he did some more fighting). Built castle at Angers and many other fortified places in the Loire. If you say "Foulques Nerra" when you see any rude fortress reminding you of Angers, you will gain a reputation as an architectural expert.

1066 Normans invade England, win Battle of Hastings, and settle. Later, a new language, English, evolves, a mixture of French and Anglo-Saxon with the hard bits left out.

1135 Loire man, Stephen (Etienne in French) count of Blois, usurps the crown of England—Matilda, daughter of Henry I, should have been queen.

1154 Loire man, Henri Plantagenet, becomes king of England as Henri II. He is the son of Matilda and Geoffrey Plantagenet, the count of Anjou. At Beaugency the French king Louis VII divorces his wife Eleanor (for misconduct). In her own right she is duchess of Aquitaine and countess of Poitou. Henry II marries her, thus acquiring a large additional part of France. He conquers Ireland and rules from the north of England to the Pyrenees. Of all his residences he prefers Chinon.

1189 Henry II dies at Chinon, and is buried at Fontevraud. His son, Richard Coeur de Lion, becomes king of England.

1199 Death of Richard Coeur de Lion. He is buried at Fontev-raud. Succeeded by his brother John, whose French possessions are thereafter confiscated.

1204 Death of Eleanor, mother of Richard and John. She too is buried at Fontevraud.

1337 Hundred Years' War begins between French and English. (Soon, Edward III of England and his son, the Black Prince, beat the French at Crécy and Poitiers, and take Calais. But towards the end of his 50-year reign Edward loses most of his French possessions).

1340 Naval battle of Sluys. England wins, so Hundred Years' War is fought in France, not in England.

1415 Henry V (Plantagenet) of England beats the French at Agincourt. He marries the French king's daughter, Cather-ine, and is declared heir to the throne of France. In 1420 he enters Paris in triumph as regent. (Henry dies in 1422; his widow Catherine marries a Welshman, Owen Tudor; their grandson, later Henry VII, becomes the first Tudor king of England).

1429 Joan of Arc meets French king Charles VII at Chinon (the English are in Paris). She ends the English siege of Orléans.

1431 Joan of Arc burnt at Rouen as a heretic by the French, though with some English influence. Charles VII makes no effort to defend her. Henry VI of England marries Marga-ret of Anjou.

1453 Last event in the Hundred Years' War: French victory at Castillon. England has only Calais left.

1461–1483 Reign of "sinister" Louis XI, fond of the Loire val-ley. Buried at Cléry-St.-André, near Orléans (his cranium, and his wife's, are in the crypt; shown on demand).

1483–1498 Reign of "affable" Charles VIII. He was born at Amboise (where he also died after banging his head against a low door; his heart is buried at Cléry-St.-André). In 1491 he married Anne, duchess of Brittany; this was an important political marriage (see Langeais in gazetteer).

1492 Columbus discovers America.

1498–1515 Reign of Louis XII, the "People's Father." He pre-fers to live at Blois. He divorces to marry Charles VIII's widow, Anne, thus keeping control of Brittany. After her death he marries the sister of Henry VIII of England.

1499 Rabelais born at Chinon.

1509–1547 Henry VIII king of England.

1515–1547 François I king of France. Prefers to live at Am-

The porcupine
Emblem of
Louis XII

The ermine
Emblem of
Anne of Brittany

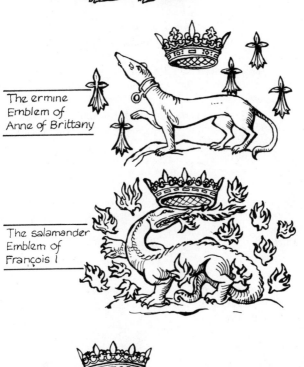

The salamander
Emblem of
François I

The pierced swan
Emblem of
Claude of France

boise, where he creates an immensely elegant court. Courtly Loire life is at its peak.

1519 Leonardo da Vinci dies at Amboise. François I had brought him there some years before as artistic and architectural adviser.

1520 François I and Henry VIII hold summit conference near Calais (Field of the Cloth of Gold). But François fails to gain English support against Habsburg empire (Spain, Austria, Netherlands) of Charles V of Spain.

1522 Joachim du Bellay ("*Heureux qui comme Ulysse a fait un beau voyage...*") born at Liré, near Champtocaux. With Ronsard ("*Allons, mignons, voir si la rose ...*"), born at La Possonière, near Vendôme, founds important literary group, La Pléiade.

1534 Jacques Cartier exploring Canada.

1547–1559 Henri II king of France. (Confusion is always caused when tourist literature misguidedly translates "Henri II" as "Henry II," the 12th-century English king who lived at Chinon in the Loire). Henri II's wife is Catherine de Médicis (1519–1589), one of the Médicis of Florence. His mistress, Diane de Poitiers, has more influence than Catherine, but Catherine gains her revenge later (see 1560–1574 below).

1553–1558 Mary Tudor (Bloody Mary) queen of England. She is a Catholic and marries Philip II of Spain. Loses Calais to the French.

1558–1603 Elizabeth I queen of England.

1559–1560 François II, son of Henri II and Catherine de Médicis, king of France. He marries Mary Stuart (Mary, queen of Scots, a niece of Henry VIII). He dies at Orléans aged 17. Mary returns to Scotland: tragic life (she is executed in 1587).

1560–1574 Reign of Charles IX of France. He is only 10 years old on coming to the throne (and only 23 when he dies). His mother, Catherine de Médicis, is regent for three years, wielding great power and influence. She is a controversial figure, very anti-Protestant.

1562–1598 Wars of religion between Catholics and Protestants.

1572 St. Batholomew's Day Massacre of Protestants in Paris, largely inspired by Catherine de Médicis.

1574–1589 Henri III king of France, another son of Catherine de Médicis. Has the duc de Guise murdered at Blois in 1588.

1589–1610 Henri IV king of France. A Protestant, he becomes a Catholic to get the throne, saying "Paris is well worth a mass." He is the first king of the Bourbon line. They are less involved with the Loire valley than their predecessors were. The valley loses its political importance.

1598 Edict of Nantes guarantees liberty of Protestants.

1608 Champlain founds Quebec.

1685 Louis XIV revokes Edict of Nantes. Many Protestants emigrate.

1699 Louisiana (named after Louis XIV) colonized by French, after exploration by Cavelier de la Salle, who went from Canada to the mouth of the Mississippi.

1776 American colonists declare Independence, their successful revolt against Britain helped by Frenchmen Lafayette and Rochambeau.

1789 French Revolution. It is followed by the Terror, and then the rise of Napoleon and general European war.

1803 Napoleon sells Louisiana to the U.S.A.

1805 Battle of Trafalgar: the French navy is defeated by Nelson and Napoleon cannot invade England.

1815 Battle of Waterloo: Napoleon is defeated and exiled.

1832 Steam navigation starts on the Loire (and ends in 1862 after competition from the railways).

1870–1871 Franco-Prussian War.

1914–1918 World War I.

1939–1945 World War II. France defeated by Nazi Germany in 1940. The Loire is liberated by the Allies and the French Resistance in August and September 1944.

1952 First *son-et-lumière* show, at Chambord.

1963 France's first atomic power station opens, at Chinon.

LOIRE GAZETTEER

Amboise

Orientation

Amboise is a bustling picturesque little town, located on the south side of the Loire, about midway between Tours and Blois on D751. The town is crowded with locals from the surrounding villages doing their shopping—especially on Friday and Sunday mornings, when there are good markets—and with tourists from all over the world who come to see the château that dominates the town and the river.

Below the château is the southern end of the bridge across the Loire, and here traffic jams worthy of much bigger towns may be observed with amusement by strollers along the wide riverside promenade, or with sweaty impatience by drivers waiting to get to the other side. This bridge is in two parts: there is an island in the middle of the river, with an excellent campsite. Indeed Amboise is a good center for campers, who, in common with other self-caterers visiting here, will find many tempting food shops along rue Nationale, a narrow pedestrians-only street running parallel to the riverside quai Général de Gaulle. There are a number of *gîtes* available in the villages to the north, highly suitable for visitors with cars if they want a base for exploration and can stay for a week or two: a glance at the map will show the riches to be found within an easy hour's drive. For short stays, there are hotels in all categories, not to mention restaurants, pizzerias, *crêperies,* snack bars, ice-cream sellers, and even purveyors of hot dogs—*le hot dog* in French. In fact Amboise is a bit too touristic for some tastes, especially in the summer when the great air-conditioned buses disgorge their international freight.

Day visitors should park on the south, or château side, of the river. If the parking lots (with meters) near the bridge are full, free parking can usually be found a few hundred yards along the river in either direction.

History and Highlights

The history of Amboise is really the history of its château. The flat-topped hill on which it stands was a Stone Age settlement, fortified in the Iron Age by a ditch and rampart, making a defensive area of some 130 acres. Very early, the river was bridged here. The fortress and town thus became of great strategic importance. Clovis, king of the Franks, met Alaric, king of the Visigoths, in about 503 on the island where the campsite now is. Of course, the Normans did their routine sacking and pillaging, destroying the fortress more than once.

The 15th and 16th centuries were Amboise's golden age. The château, enlarged and embellished, was a royal residence. Charles VII, the king Joan of Arc tried to ginger up, stayed here. Louis XI's children were born here. Charles VIII banged his head on a low doorway—you will be shown it—and died. Louis XII preferred Blois, but François I, who came to the throne in 1515, and whose long nose is seen in so many pictures in various châteaux, made it the main base for his brilliant and luxurious court. In 1560, the 15-year-old François II settled here with his wife, Mary, queen of Scots, and his mother, Catherine de Médicis. An ill-planned Protestant plot—the Amboise Conspiracy—against him failed, and visitors will be shown where the corpses of 1,200 condemned conspirators dangled from the walls.

Later, a decline set in. Demolitions took place before and after the Revolution. What was left of the château became a barracks and a button factory. At the end of the last century efforts were made to conserve what remained. This was less than a third of its former extent, but still, as will be seen, quite a lot. Since 1974 the St.-Louis Foundation, under the count of Paris, has been looking after the château. The count is the claimant to the French crown: if France became a monarchy again, would Amboise be the royal palace?

The Château

Open daily except Christmas Day and New Year's Day 9–12, 2–6:30 Sept. to June, and 9–6:30 July and August. Keep your ticket, which you buy at the entrance to the grounds; it entitles you to a guided tour of the interior. The *entrée du château* is signposted.

One cannot do better than quote Henry James, who came by train from Tours just over 100 years ago:

> The great point is to go . . . on a day when the great view of the Loire, which you enjoy from the battlements and terraces, presents itself under a friendly sky . . . We spent the greater part of a perfect Sunday morning looking at it . . . The interior is virtually a blank . . . A worthy woman with a military profile attended us . . . Sweet

Amboise

was the view, and magnificent; we preferred it so much to certain
portions of the interior, and to occasional effusions of historical information, that the old lady with the profile sometimes lost patience with
us. We laid ourselves open to the charge of preferring it even to the
little chapel of St. Hubert, which stands on the edge of the great
terrace and has, over the portal, a wonderful sculpture . . . In the
matter of position Amboise is certainly supreme in the list of perched
places . . . The platforms, the bastions, the terraces, the high-niched
windows and balconies, the hanging gardens and dizzy crenelations
of this complicated structure, keep you in perpetual intercourse with
the immense horizon . . .

Today, instead of the military lady, there is a posse of guides
—only some of whom speak English, but leaflets in English can
be borrowed—who will trot you round the interior. This has
been furnished, in parts, and is on the whole worth the 40
minutes the tour takes, especially as only with the guided visit
can you get inside the great round tower. Instead of a staircase
it has a spiral ramp, "so wide and gradual," says James, "that
a coach and four may be driven to the top," or, today, a small
car.

James's advice is good. It would be a pity to go on a dull rainy
day instead of luxuriating in the view in the sun, the bright flags
waving in the breeze, the river glinting. Even if you don't want
to take the guided tour, you are still free, having bought your
ticket, to stroll around the grounds and take your time admiring
the well-restored chapel of St.-Hubert and the splendid carvings
above its doorway: the Virgin and Child, with Charles VIII and
his wife Anne of Brittany kneeling in prayer and, below, the
miraculous hunt of St.-Hubert (who was converted to Christian-
ity by an uncatchable stag with a shining cross in its antlers). This
is where Leonardo da Vinci's bones are said to lie.

Other Sights

The Clos-Lucé. Opening times same as the château. Visits are
unguided (leaflets in English), but there is a helpful guide if
wanted (and if he has the time). Allow anything from 30 minutes
for a visit.

No visitor to Amboise should omit this delightful Renaissance
manor house. It was lent by François I to Leonardo da Vinci,
who spent the last four years of his life here, dying in 1519. It
was opened as a private museum by its owner in 1955. You can
wander freely without a guide, from room to room, all of them
interestingly furnished. It's no more than five minutes' walk

from the château, up the rue Victor Hugo, a narrow street with troglodytic houses.

The Clos-Lucé boasts a pleasant chapel, added by Charles VIII in 1490 for Anne of Brittany. Otherwise, the house is an admirable Renaissance gentleman's residence, from Leonardo's bedroom down to the kitchens where he used to warm himself on winter evenings.

In the basement there's an extraordinary exhibit. Leonardo was not only a painter and sculptor of genius. His notebooks are full of ideas for inventions. Most of them were impracticable in his day, though feasible with the right materials and technology. I.B.M. has constructed large models here, using Leonardo's plans and descriptions: three-speed gearboxes; a flying machine; a steam cannon, the cannon ball propelled when water is vaporized on white-hot metal; a parachute; a military tank; a clockwork motor car; a swing bridge. Here they are, a fascinating collection, with descriptions in French and English.

The house can be rather crowded, especially when bus-loads of Italian school kids are doing the Leonardo pilgrimage. For a quiet ramble through it in the summer, it's best to come as soon as possible after the morning opening time.

There is a pleasant garden running down to a stream; a modest snack bar in the grounds (open weekends only Sept.–June, daily July and Aug.); postcards of Leonardo's drawings and models are sold.

Musée de la Poste, rue Joyeuse (near the château, though poorly signposted). Open daily except Tues., most public holidays and Dec., 9:30–12 and 2–6 in summer, 10–12 and 2–5 in winter. Leaflets in English are lent.

If you have an hour to spare in Amboise, after visiting the château and the Clos-Lucé, it would be a pity not to come here. The terms "post" and *"poste"* are rather misleading. The modern postal system developed from the days when relays of horses were kept at staging "posts." Travelers by post-chaise and stage coach changed horses there, with postillions taking the used horses back to the "post" that was their home. (This is why so many Hôtels de la Poste in France have garage space: they were the former stables). And of course dispatch riders changed horses at these posts, taking precedence over ordinary travelers.

The museum is in a heavily restored 16th-century house. It is an agreeable muddle of all sorts of things, through which you can wander freely. On the first floor is the "horse post" section: models of stage coaches, postillions' accoutrements, prints,

drawings, photographs, postmasters' certificates with royal sig-
natures, whips, pistols, saddles, maps.

Upstairs is the "letter post" section, with an equally fascinating and often amusingly odd collection of objects. Postage
stamps, of course, and old envelopes, but especially pictures
and prints. To single out just one exhibit: there is a set of cards
from the last century showing 100 postmen from all nations.
The British and French ones are very smart, in a Victorian way,
but the American ones seem straight out of Huck Finn. Transport by sea and air—and by balloon, during the siege of Paris—
only loosely connected with *la poste* is randomly represented;
there is a goodly number of posters of transatlantic liners on the
top floor.

Hotels and Restaurants

Château de Pray (E), on D751 (signposted), (tel. 47–57–23–
67). 16 rooms, all with bath or shower. Closed Jan. to mid-Feb.
Located a mile or so out of Amboise, this is a real château, with
all the lordliness of François I's time, including a 25-acre park,
and with a terrace overlooking the river.

Le Choiseul (E), 36 quai Charles-Guinot (tel. 47–30–45–45).
20 rooms, all with bath or shower. Closed early Jan. to mid-
Mar. The best hotel in town, nicely situated on the Loire below
the château, with a good restaurant.

Lion d'Or (M), 17 quai Charles-Guinot (tel. 47–57–00–23). 22
rooms, all with bath or shower. Garage. Open mid-Mar. to end
Oct. Similar location to Le Choiseul above, and a pleasant medium-priced hotel, with probably the best restaurant in Amboise,
though only if you choose the more expensive *menus* and
wines.

Novotel (M), rue des Sablonnières (tel. 47–57–42–07). 82
rooms, all with bath or shower. Modern hotel, with all facilities,
including a swimming pool, about a mile out of town. A reliable
member of the Novotel chain.

La Brèche (I), 26 rue Jules-Ferry (tel. 47–57–00–79). 15 rooms,
some only with bath or shower. Garage. Closed Dec. to mid-
Jan; restaurant closed Sat. evening and all day Sun. from Oct.
to Easter. About 100 yards from the rail station and thus on the
"wrong," north, side of the river, but highly satisfactory given
the low rates.

Fast Facts

Tourist Office: *Office du Tourisme,* quai Général de Gaulle (tel. 47–57–09–28). Efficiently run, with English speaking staff.

Tours: The tourist office organizes walks around the town, starting from the Town Hall, in July and Aug.

Son et Lumière: Daily at the château in July and Aug.

Angers

Orientation

Angers, the capital of Anjou, is one of the three major towns of the Loire valley (Tours and Orléans are the others). It lies on the little river Maine, just to the north of the Loire itself, toward the western end of the Loire valley. Nantes and the Atlantic are 89 km. (55 miles) to the west, Tours and Orléans 106 km. (66 miles) and 210 km. (130 miles) respectively to the east. Lying toward the western end of the Loire, Angers, though itself a town of considerable interest, is not an ideal center for exploring the region. Saumur, 45 km. (28 miles) upstream, for example, makes a better base, especially for car drivers wishing to take in the other major sites: Fontevraud, Chinon, Azay-le-Rideau, and so on.

The town arouses contradictory feelings. The poet Joachim du Bellay, languishing in 16th-century Rome, sighed for *"la douceur Angevine,"* the Angevin sweetness. But 100 years ago Henry James thought Angers was, "a sell." He admitted that the château was "worth a pilgrimage," but, "one good look does your business," and there was nothing to see inside. (Things are different now). He dismissed the cathedral rapidly—and felt guilty later—and spent most of his time in a café waiting for a train. Henry wasn't at his best that day.

Picking up other books, you find similarly divided views. Love it or leave it. But no one can deny that the château is a perfect specimen of great, grim, massive defensiveness; nor that the tourist office is a model of helpfulness, showering the visitor with suggestions for visits, excursions and activities—many of them having nothing to do with historical monuments, which may be a relief to some—to fill happily a stay of several days.

Whether staying a morning or a week, aim first for the château. The tourist office is opposite in the place Kennedy. As well as their leaflets and free town plan, pick up the combined, money-saving ticket for the château, the cathedral treasury, and other museums and galleries around town. There's a parking lot just by the tourist office. If, as is only too likely, it's full, don't try driving up the narrow streets towards the cathedral, many of which are in any case for pedestrians only, but rejoin the main boulevards: there are plenty of well signposted lots elsewhere. Alternatively, head across the river and park there.

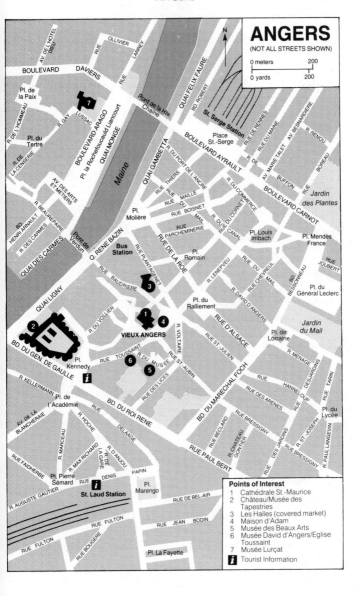

ANGERS
(NOT ALL STREETS SHOWN)

0 meters 200
0 yards 200

Points of Interest
1 Cathédrale St.-Maurice
2 Château/Musée des
 Tapestries
3 Les Halles (covered market)
4 Maison d'Adam
5 Musée des Beaux Arts
6 Musée David d'Angers/Eglise
 Toussaint
7 Musée Lurçat
i Tourist Information

The Château

Open daily except most public holidays, Oct. to June 9:30–12 and 2–6, July, Aug. and Sept. 9:30–6. Allow about two hours for a visit.

Across the château's dry moat, where flowers bloom and deer graze, the horizontally striped, dark-shale and limestone walls and bastion glower at you. Foulques Nerra started it, but Louis IX—St.-Louis—not to be confused with the sinister Louis XI—did the main work, from 1228 to 1238. Once over the drawbridge, you surprisingly find yourself in a pleasant medieval-type garden, with a graceful 16th-century, white tufa-stone chapel beyond the trim yews, a peaceful contrast to the fortress walls around. Climb up one of the great towers, the Tour du Moulin, and reflect on the passing centuries this place has seen, from fortress to barracks, and then munitions stores during the Nazi occupation. Luckily, the Germans moved the explosives out just before an Allied air raid (the chapel suffered some damage, but has been neatly repaired).

And then, still in the grounds of the château, you come to a new building, blending skillfully with the old, housing the *Tapestry of the Apocalypse*. This extraordinary series of illustrations, depicting the last book of the Bible, Revelations, is macabre, sometimes horrifying—mountains of fire falling from heaven while boats capsize and men struggle in the water—and sometimes amusing: the seven-headed beast has a certain charm. When it was finished in 1390 it was all of 540 feet long and 16½ feet high. A third of it has disappeared, but you can still see the remaining 360 feet at your own speed, and in comfort. There are leaflets in English. Opposite each tapestry panel is the corresponding verse from the Bible, though in French only. Souvenirs, from postcards to coffee-table books, are on sale.

Other Sights

Cathédrale St.-Maurice. A substantial Gothic cathedral, dating from the 12th and 13th centuries and notable principally for its spectacular facade and stained glass, a good deal of which is original though there are also many latter additions, including massive specimens of gloomy 19th-century woodwork. The treasure room has superb exhibits.

Maison d'Adam, rue St.-Aubin. A remarkable half-timbered 15th-century house hard among the shops, restaurants and cafés that line the pretty, traffic-free center. It's decorated with a bizarre series of carvings, including one of Adam and Eve, hence the name.

Angers: The Lady of Rohan tapestry

Musée des Beaux Arts, 10 rue Musée (tel. 41–88–64–65). Open daily except Mon. 10–12 and 2–6. Located in the late 15th-century Logis Barrault, where Caesar Borgia, Mary Queen of Scots, and Catherine de Médicis stayed. A surprisingly good collection of Old Masters—Raphael, Watteau, Boucher, Fragonard, Corot—constitute the main attraction.

Musée David d'Angers, 33 rue Toussaint (tel. 41–88–64–65). Open daily except Mon. 10–12 and 2–6. What was originally a ruined church—the église Toussaint—has now, with its new glass roof, become a museum housing works by David, whose home town has become part of his name, a sculptor of prominence in the 19th century but not much in fashion now.

Musée Lurçat, Hospice St.-Jean, blvd. Arago. Open daily except Mon. and public holidays 10–12 and 2–6. This beautiful medieval hospital, on the other side of the river from the town, houses another tapestry, *The Song of the World.* It's a modern work, a "mere" 255 feet long, designed by Jean Lurçat, who has revived the art of tapestry in France; admired by some, not by others.

Excursions

Detailed information on all trips to and around Angers is available from the tourist office. Among the most popular are balloon trips—it sounds even more appealing in French: a hot-air balloon is a *Montgolfière*. These take place in the summer and fall, weather permitting, first thing in the morning or in the evening. A bus follows to pick you up wherever you come down. These trips are expensive, however, and should be booked at least a week in advance. Less spectacular but much cheaper bus tours, lasting either a full day or just half a day, can also be arranged; these will generally take in a number of châteaux nearby and probably wine tasting as well. Cruises on the Loire, with lunch on board, are also a regular feature. Boats can also be hired for as short a time as a day or two—though longer if desired—but not on the Loire, which is felt to be too demanding for amateur navigators. The tourist office will also supply itineraries for car drivers.

An enjoyable visit can be made to the Cointreau factory, where the well-known liqueur is made—the visit is well organized. Do not omit the Maison du Vin, near the tourist office, an outlet for local wine producers. A great many admirable wines are made around here: Rosé d'Anjou, Coteaux du Layon, Quarts de Chaume, Savennières, and the sparkling white, almost champagne-like wines of Saumur. There's free tasting for suitably respectable-looking visitors and lots of information, particularly on wine producers in the region to visit: a good booklet suggests enough circuits to last a strong-headed wine enthusiast a week, though these drives are pleasant enough even if you don't touch a drop. They can also, if you're lucky, make appointments for visits to the Château de la Roche-aux-Moines, where the Joly family—and well they might be—make one of the top six wines in the whole country, Coulée de Serrant.

Hotels

Mercure (E), pl. Mendes-France (tel. 41–60–34–81). 86 rooms, all with bath or shower. Garage. Modern and comfortable hotel, reliable in almost every way, a good 20 minutes' walk from the château next to the Jardin des Plantes. Has a reasonable restaurant.
Anjou (M), 1 blvd. Foch (tel. 41–88–24–82). 51 rooms, all with bath. Garage. An older, but modernized hotel by the Jardin du Mail, not too far from the château. Its medium-priced restaurant, the Salamandre, can be safely recommended.

Univers (I), rue de la Gare (tel. 41–88–43–58). 45 rooms, some with bath or shower. By the rail station, about 10 minutes' walk from the château. Breakfast, but no restaurant.

There is a luxurious **campsite** at the Lac de Maine leisure center, with electricity, beach, sailing, tennis, and restaurant.

Restaurants

Angers abounds in decent restaurants, but none that is likely to tempt the French connoisseur out of his way to worship at. Most of the hotels have restaurants—see above—but you might also try:

Le Toussaint (M), 7 rue Toussaint (tel. 41–87–46–20). Closed Aug., Sun. and Mon. Close to the cathedral, serving excellent *nouvelle cuisine* mostly based on local specialties.

Les Halles (I). Closed Mon. Food market in the shadow of the cathedral where, in addition to wandering around the displays, you can get a good, not too expensive lunch at tables in front of one of the stalls: oysters, sole *meunière,* cheese or fruit; or just a snack of a dozen oysters; or one of those enormous *plateaux de fruits de mer* (assorted shellfish, all spanking fresh).

Taverne Kanter (I), Les Halles. One of a restaurant chain that stretches across France; in the first floor of the food market. Recommended for a quick, inexpensive meal: steak and french fries, and *choucroute*—sauerkraut with sausages and ham—are specialties.

Fast Facts

Tourist Office: pl. Kennedy (tel. 41–88–69–93). Includes a branch of the Accueil de France organization, who will make hotel reservations for you anywhere in France, though not more than five days in advance.

Car Hire: *Avis,* 13 rue Max Richard (tel. 41–88–20–24); *Europcar,* 26 blvd. du Général de Gaulle (tel. 41–88–80–80); *Inter-Rent,* 30 rue Denis Papin (tel. 41–88–54–44).

Azay-le-Rideau

Orientation

Twenty-eight km. (20 miles) southwest of Tours on N152 and just a few miles south of the Loire itself, Azay-le-Rideau lies on the banks of the little river Indre. A visit here is easily combined with one to Saché, six km. (four miles) to the southeast, crossing the Indre either at Azay-le-Rideau or at Saché; there are bridges at both and both roads are picturesque. Villaines-les-Rochers is similarly easily reached, along D17 or D57; it too is about six km. away, almost due south of Azay-le-Rideau. Villandry is about 11 km. (seven miles) to the north, reached on the little D39 via Vallères.

A visit to Azay-le-Rideau means a visit to the château here, the little village having become dominated by the tourist industry; Azay is very much on the tourist bus routes.

The Château

Open daily 9:15–12 and 2–6:30 in summer, 9:30–12 and 2–4:45 in winter. Allow 45 minutes for the guided visit of the interior. Leaflets in English available.

"Magical," "a jewel," "ravishing," "a most perfect and beautiful thing." The writers agree about this white, fairy-tale château, mirrored in the waters of its moat. It was built by a royal financier, Berthelot, from 1518 to 1529. These dates mean there is nothing military about it. It is a pure Renaissance pleasure palace. Its turrets and machicolations are just for fun. It was Berthelot's wife, Philippe, who was in charge of the building. Like Chenonceau, planned by Catherine Briçonnet, it radiates bygone feminine grace and delicacy.

Financiers under François I might have been able to make their pile, but they led a risky life. Berthelot had to flee France following a financial scandal almost the moment the château was complete. Many lucky owners succeeded him, until, in 1905, the State bought it.

The outside is so enchanting that you think the interior must be a dream of delight. Not quite. The usual guided trudge and lecture on history, with a leaflet in English, the usual random sprinkling of oddments of furniture from different periods (there is a good painting of Gabrielle d'Estrées, Henri IV's mistress, but you can study it better in reproductions than where it hangs

Azay-le-Rideau

here). Put it another way, if this is the only château you visit, then the interior is worth a look, but if you know Chenonceau and Chambord and Cheverny, you will have seen better interiors and furnishings, and more pleasurably.

Some years ago it was possible to get into the attractive park free, through the little chapel. But this has been stopped now. For a leisured close look at the outside you must pay at the entrance, as for the full visit. Entrancing views can, it's true, be stolen from the bridge leading to the Chinon road, over the Indre. But they will tempt the hard-up visitor to pay the fee and get nearer.

Lunch Spots

The village has good genuine *charcuteries* and *pâtisseries* for buying picnic-makings. There is also a good local wine. Opposite the château entrance there is a simple cafe, the **Salamandre**—the salamander, turning up on fireplaces at Azay and almost every other château, was the emblem of François I— adequate for steak and french fries at lowish tourist prices.

There's also an excellent gourmet restaurant at Saché; see page 124.

Fast Facts

Tourist Office: 26 rue Gambetta (tel. 47–43–34–40). Open mid-Mar. to mid-Sept. only.

Son et Lumière: A delightful *son et lumière* is put on in the château grounds on summer nights. Details from the tourist office.

Beaugency

Orientation

This picturesque town of about 7,500 Balgentians, as the inhabitants are called, slopes steeply to its 16th-century bridge over the Loire. It contains nothing of outstanding importance, and can be omitted by visitors in a hurry. But it makes a good base for people who do not want to stay in the bigger towns; both Orléans and Blois are less than 30 km. (18 miles) away, and many places of note are well within a lazy hour's drive or less. The A10 highway can be joined 10 km. (six miles) away, near Meung; from there it's only 91 km. (55 miles) to Tours and 145 km. (87 miles) to Paris. The railway station is on the main Paris–Tours line.

Sights

The **Church of Notre-Dame,** where three archbishops and a throng of bishops and lesser clerics annulled Louis VII's marriage to Eleanor of Aquitaine—while she waited at Tavers to marry Henry Plantagenet (Henry II) and thus enable him to rule England and most of France—still stands, though it has seen troubles. It had to be re-roofed in wood (faking stone) in 1567 after damage by rioting Huguenot soldiers; and German shells destroyed the windows in 1940. Nearby, the **Tour de César** is a massive 11th-century tower which Joan of Arc had great difficulty taking from Talbot's garrison.

The **Château Dunois** houses a good regional museum, with costumes, peasant furniture and other curiosities. Open daily April to Sept. 9–12 and 2–6; other months daily, except Tues., 9–12 and 2–4. Guided visit; leaflet in English. Tel. 38–44–55–23.

Hotels

L'Abbaye (E), quai Abbaye (tel. 38–44–67–35). 13 rooms, 5 suites. A former abbey tastefully modernized, with splendid views of the bridge and the river. Excellent gourmet restaurant.
La Tonnellerie (E), Tavers (tel. 38–44–68–15). Three km. (two miles) outside town on N152. Peaceful and luxurious, with meals in the gardens in good weather.
Ecu de Bretagne (I), pl. Martroi (tel. 38–44–67–60). 26 rooms with bath or shower. Closed late Jan. through Feb. A good hotel

and restaurant on the main square, more traditional and less expensive.

There is a well-equipped **campsite** with shady trees near the river. Open April through Sept.

Fast Facts

Tourist Office: 28 pl. Martroi (tel. 38–44–54–42). Open May through Oct.

Festivals: There is a fair in May, an antique fair in June and a wine fair in Sept. Market day is Saturday.

Beauregard

Orientation

Although Beauregard is only nine km. (five miles) from Blois on D956 and six km. (four miles) from Cheverny on D765, few people visit this small château. It has two extraordinary rooms, one big and one small, which are a joy to tour without a crowd. If you arrive by the country road that comes from the village of Cellettes, consider packing a lunch to eat in the shady picnic area outside the château gates.

The Château

Open daily April through Sept. 9:30–12 and 2–6:30; daily except Wed. mid-Feb through March and Oct. to mid-Jan. 9:30–12 and 2–5; closed mid-Jan. to mid-Feb. Guided visit; leaflets in English. More information from Blois tourist office. Tel. 54–70–40–05.

The crowning attraction of Beauregard is its Galerie des Illustres, or Gallery of the Famous. Round the walls of this mammoth room are life-size portraits of over 300 celebrities from the 14th century to the early 17th. The effect is harmonious and civilized. Henry VIII and Anne Boleyn are there, as well as Thomas More, Cardinal Wolsey, Queen Elizabeth I and her admirer the earl of Essex; so is the Dutch Count Egmont, subject of the Beethoven overture; and hundreds of French luminaries, of course. This unique gallery was begun by Paul Ardier, who bought Beauregard after having been a top civil servant for 55 years. His son and granddaughter continued his work, and little in the room has changed since their day. The floor is paved with over 5,000 Delft tiles, all different, depicting an army on the march. The blue hand-painted tiles are precious and fragile; visitors are asked to keep to the straw-matted walkways.

The next stop is the tiny Cabinet des Grelots, the *grelots* in question being little round bells, created for an earlier owner whose coat-of-arms included three of them. This study, or library, is entirely paneled, ceiling and all, with intricately carved and gilded oak. One set of panels depicts the occupations of man: love, war, music, painting and of course tennis.

Other highlights include an interesting kitchen, in use from 1520 to 1969. The present owners use a more modern one.

Béhuard and Environs

Orientation

Béhuard is a two-mile-long island in the Loire 15 km. (nine miles) southwest of Angers on D111. It's not only a charming place in itself; it's also convenient to a half-dozen other minor attractions within a half-hour's drive. More information on the Béhuard area is available at the Angers tourist office.

Sights

Béhuard. On a good day, Béhuard is green and smiling, with cows basking in fruit orchards under the warm Angevin sun. The island can be grim as well, when the treacherous Loire is flooding during the rainy season, but you won't be reach it in that case—notices reading "Route Barrée: Inondation" will bar the low-lying lanes leading to the bridges.

Prudent boatmen have never disdained help from any quarter on this stretch of the river. Béhuard was the site of an early pagan sanctuary dedicated to a river god; in the 5th century it became a Christian chapel. After Louis XI was saved from shipwreck here in the 15th century, he ordered a church to be built on the same site, in gratitude to the Virgin Mary. Built into a rock-face, it is a tiny church and a pretty one; its roof is in the shape of an overturned boat.

The village, with its 93 inhabitants, is pretty, but has been discovered. Souvenirs are on sale, of course, and the little café that gave such good value for simple fare 20 years ago now caters to the tripper from Angers.

Rochefort-sur-Loire. Three km. (two miles) south of Béhuard, this pretty little town of 2,000 inhabitants stands on the river Louet and makes a good stopping-point for those interested in spending a night in the Béhuard region. Rochefort's main square is sedate and charming, fronted by colorful, turreted residences.

St.-Lambert-du-Lattay. This village can be reached by traveling nine km. (six miles) due south from Rochefort, or 23 km. (14 miles) southwest of Angers on N160. The most picturesque drive takes you 15 km. (nine miles) southeast from Chalonnes on D961 and D17. St.-Lambert lies in the heart of the Coteaux du Layon wine district; here, wine-makers' cellars offer tastings and well-marked footpaths meander about the vineyards. There is a good little wine museum—**La Musée de la Vigne et du**

Vin. Open daily July and Aug. from 2:30; Sat. and Sun. afternoons May, June, Sept. and Oct.

Château de la Roche aux Moines. Opposite Béhuard on the
north bank of the Loire is the pretty town of Savennières, with
well-preserved windmills. A short way along the road to Angers
is the **Château de la Roche aux Moines,** where King John of
England suffered one of his many defeats. More importantly,
perhaps, it is the home of one of the world's best—and most
expensive—wines: the Coulée de Serrant. Pilgrims will be able
to buy a bottle or two; avid wine-tasters should make appointments for wine-tastings through the Maison du Vin in Angers.

Château de Serrant. Eight km. (five miles) along the little
D311, or seven km. (four miles) due north of Chalonnes on
D961 is the village of St.-Georges-sur-Loire, just outside of
which, on the road to Angers, is the Château de Serrant. Open
daily except Tues., April through Oct. 9–11:30 and 2–6; no
Tues. closing July and Aug. Guided visit; leaflet in English. Tel.
41–39–13–01.

Although it has nothing to do with the Serrant wines, the
Château de Serrant is every bit as sumptuous. Built in the 16th,
17th and 18th centuries, it houses some fine tapestries and
furniture. It was bought in 1749 by Francis Walsh, descendant
of one of the "Wild Geese"—the Irish who fled their country
with the Stuarts after the Battle of the Boyne. The Walshes made
a fortune in business at Nantes, and it was Francis's son Antoine
who carried Bonnie Prince Charlie to Scotland in his frigate in
1745. A picture in the library commemorates this ill-starred
good turn.

Hotel

Le Grand Hotel (I), rue Gasnier, Rochefort-sur-Loire (tel. 41–
78–70–06). 8 rooms with shower. Closed mid-Jan. to mid-Feb.,
last week in June, and Sun. evenings and Mon. except July and
Aug. Despite the name, it's a modest place with simple bedrooms and fine local food.

Blois

Orientation

It is worth coming from the ends of the earth to spend a couple of days in Blois, provided your hill- and stair-climbing muscles are in good shape. Steep and quaint, Blois is the most attractive of the major cities on the Loire, and once there you'll be tempted to extend your stay. It's also a convenient touring center; a quick glance at the map shows how many places of interest are nearby. There are slow, scenic drives along the roads on the north and south banks of the river, and the A10 highway is just outside town, giving easy access to Tours, Orléans and Paris.

Blois is on the main train line to Paris; there are local trains to several places of interest. The bus office, Autocars STD, is at place Victor-Hugo. It provides timetables for regular bus services to nearby towns, such as Montrichard, Vendôme and Beaugency.

The most pleasant way to approach Blois is from the south bank of the Loire, admiring the skyline of towers and steeples and the charming 18th-century bridge rising to a pinnacle in the middle. The bridge leads into the main shopping street, rue Denis Papin, named after the Huguenot who became a refugee in England after the revocation of the Edict of Nantes in 1685 and invented the pressure cooker. If you're arriving by car, aim for the Parking des Lices, a big, free parking lot; if you're coming from Amboise or points west, follow the signs saying "Château, Office du Tourisme". There is a parking lot in front of the château, but it is expensive and often full.

The Château

Open daily 9–12 and 2–5 or 6:30; no mid-day closing May through Aug. Optional guided visit; English speaking guides, leaflets in English. Allow 45 minutes for guided tour, not including Musée des Beaux Arts. Tel. 54–78–06–62 and 54–74–16–06.

Blois strikes the visitor immediately. Henry James, who came in 1882, wrote:

> In that soft, clear, merry light of Touraine, everything shows, everything speaks. Charming are the taste, the happy proportions, the colour of this beautiful front, to which the new feeling for a purely

Blois

domestic architecture—an architecture of security and tranquility, in which art could indulge itself—gave an air of youth and gladness.

Depressed by the military starkness of Angers, James was cheerful at Blois. Indeed, though purists complain of too much restoration, regilding and repainting, the château is a bright and happy place to visit.

Stand in the courtyard and you see several centuries around you. All that remains of the 13th century is the great hall, the Salle des Etats Généraux, and a tower, the Tour du Foix, with good views over town, river and countryside. The Renaissance blooms in the château entrance, known as the Louis XII Wing (1498–1503), and comes to full flower in the François I Wing (1515–1524), the masterpiece of which is the openwork spiral staircase, painstakingly restored. To the left is the classical Gaston d'Orléans Wing (1635–1638), much admired by connoisseurs.

The visit—guided or by yourself—starts with the staircase. At the bottom is what the French call a *diaporama,* an audiovisual display in French, tracing the history of the château. Up the splendid staircase is a series of big rooms with tremendous fireplaces decorated with the gilded porcupine, emblem of Louis XII; the ermine of Anne of Brittany; and the fire-breathing salamander of François I. The ceilings are rich and intricate, the paneling masterfully carved and gilded. In the colossal council room, the duc de Guise was murdered on the orders of Henri III. Henry James was shown every spot connected with it by "a small, shrill boy" who had "learned his lesson in perfection," but James preferred the fireplaces, saying they reminded him of "expensive 'sets' at the grand opera."

Do not miss the **Musée des Beaux Arts,** the art gallery in the Louis XII Wing. Many tourists do; it is relatively free of crowds. Entrance is included in the château fee, and there's no one to hurry or bore you. These lordly rooms include more stupendous fireplaces—with the initials L and A, for Louis and Anne—and a well-arranged collection of varied paintings. Particularly good is the 16th-century work, including a naive French *Tree of Good and Evil* and a Flemish "comic strip" of Adam and Eve in Paradise. A picture of the duchess of Angoulême passing through Blois in 1823 shows as many local worthies as possible, all with faces turned so as to be easily recognizable by their near and dear; it is delightful to see a painting which must have made many a Blois heart swell with pride. There are better pictures in these rooms, but none as amusing.

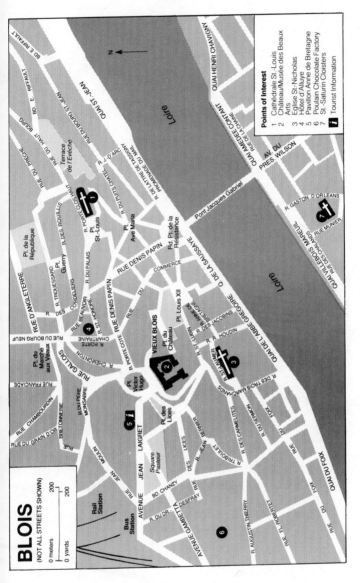

BLOIS
(NOT ALL STREETS SHOWN)

0 meters 200
0 yards 200

Points of Interest

1 Cathédrale St.-Louis
2 Château/Musée des Beaux Arts
3 Eglise St.-Nicholas
4 Hôtel d'Alluye
5 Pavillon Anne de Bretagne
6 Poulain Chocolate Factory
7 St.-Saturin Cloisters
i Tourist Information

Other Sights

Eglise St.-Nicholas. Mostly 12th-century, this majestic building is far prettier than the later and better-known Cathedral of St.-Louis. Originally part of a Benedictine Abbey, the church has lovely grounds which front on the river.

Poulain Chocolate Factory. The factory has stood here since 1848, when the raw materials were brought from Nantes in the days of Loire shipping. Visits to the factory are almost as popular as visits to the château, and include a film, a tour of the machinery, and free samples. You can reserve a spot on the tour through the tourist office or the factory itself (tel. 54–78–39–21; ask for *poste* 339).

Vieux Blois. This hilly neighborhood of ancient houses makes fascinating walking territory; a stroll, aided by the tourist office's town plan, can easily take two hours. Guided tours, some in English, start from the tourist office daily except Wed. and Sun. in July and Aug.

Hotels

Relais des Landes (E), Ouchamps, 41120 Les Montils (tel. 54–44–03–33). 18 fully equipped rooms. Open Easter through Oct. A 17th-century manor house in a park 16 km. (10 miles) from Blois. Restaurant (M) closed Wed.

Le Monarque (M), 61 rue Porte-Chartraine (tel. 54–78–02–35). 22 rooms with bath or shower.

Novotel (M), 41260 La Chausée St.-Victor (tel. 54–78–33–57). 116 rooms, fully equipped. Four km. (two miles) northeast of town on D149. Modern and efficient. Fine restaurant (M).

Anne de Bretagne (I), 31 av. Jean-Laigret (tel. 54–78–05–38). 29 rooms, some with bath or shower. Closed last two weeks in Feb. Modest, near the château. No restaurant.

Hostellerie de la Loire (I), 8 rue de Lattre de Tassigny (tel. 54–74–26–60). 17 rooms, some with bath or shower. Closed mid-Jan. to mid-Feb. and one week in June. Near the château. Restaurant (M) has good Loire wine list.

The town of Onzain, 16 km. (10 miles) away, offers many upmarket lodging possibilities. There is an adequate municipal **campsite** in Blois, on the south bank near the modern bridge. A larger and more lavishly equipped one, the **Camping-Caravanning International du Lac de Loire,** is three km. (two miles) east on the south bank.

Restaurants

There is a good café of the touristy sort in the square outside
the château. Down the steps and along some pedestrians-only
streets, rue Denis Papin is good for strolling and eating.
La Péniche (M–E), promenade du Mail. On a barge moored to
the riverbank, Germain Bosque does delicious *menu* and *à la
carte* specialties. Plenty of parking space.
Bocca d'Or (M), rue Haute. Patrice Galland serves delicate
creations in a vaulted 14th-century cellar.
Le Penalty (I), rue Denis Papin, near the riverfront. Good,
inexpensive fast food.

Fast Facts

Tourist Office: 3 av. Jean Laigret (tel. 54–74–06–49). Open
daily in tourist season 9–7; rest of year Mon. to Sat. 9–6 with
mid-day closing. English spoken. Arranges hotel bookings
throughout France, provides guides, organizes conference
facilities. Information on horse-riding, fishing, tennis, nudism,
car and bicycle rentals.
Son et Lumière: At the château most evenings April through
Sept. Details of times and dates from the château or the tourist
office; no reservations, tickets available at the château entrance.
A short but good show in French, followed by one in English.
Tours and Excursions: The tourist office makes reservations for
many excursions, including:
  ● bus trips to Chambord, Cheverny, Chenonceaux and Amboise.
  ● half-day cruises on the Loire, combined with château visits.
  ● plane flights, from a half-hour to two hours, over a number
of châteaux.
  ● circuits by helicopter over the châteaux.
  ● *montgolfière* (hot-air balloon) trips from Chambord.
Car Hire: *Avis,* 6 rue Jean Moulin (tel. 54–74–48–15); *Hertz,*
5 rue du Dr. Desfray (tel. 54–74–03–03); *Europcar,* 26–28 rue
Fénelon.

Chambord

Orientation

Chambord, 18 km. (11 miles) east of Blois, is the largest of the Loire châteaux, but it is far more than that. To omit it from a tour is not only to miss out on an awesome architectural spectacle; it is also to pass up the opportunity to join the heated controversy that surrounds it. Chambord is certainly the kind of thing William Randolph Hearst would have built if he had had enough money, but instead of moaning about ostentatious displays of wealth and power, taxpayers in the Century of the Common Man should cast off care and enjoy themselves here. Pay no attention to writers from ten years back who grumble about cheerless, empty rooms; a lot has changed since then and there is now plenty to see inside.

If you arrive by car, you won't be able to park in the miles of game preserve which surround the château. There is parking, for a small fee, on the château grounds. From here, you can amble around the outside of the château without paying to go in, unlike at Chaumont and Azay-le-Rideau for instance. To tour Chambord properly takes a long time, and the usual two-hour closing at mid-day makes planning more difficult. Still, with a short detour you can make this 20-minute stroll while en route anywhere along the south bank of the Loire between Orléans and Blois, saving the interior for another day.

The town of Chambord, with its 200 inhabitants, is as tiny as the château is massive. Those interested in night-life should stay in Blois; those interested in luxury should head to nearby Bracieux eight km. (five miles) across the game preserve. It would be unwise, however, to start from so far away that you had less than two hours to devote to the château.

History and Highlights

François I, he of the long nose and the salamanders, built most of Chambord, starting in 1519. In his enthusiasm, he wanted to have the Loire diverted to form an appropriate moat, but was persuaded—by Leonardo da Vinci, probably—to make do with the river Cosson. François I never lived in it for long periods, but used to turn up from time to time for a little hunting, with his furniture, luggage, friends, hangers-on and servants. Twelve-thousand horses were generally needed, as well as a few she-asses; ladies of the time knew that regular baths in asses' milk were good for the complexion.

Later kings made short stays according to their tastes. Charles IX and Louis XII were keen huntsmen. Louis XIV had Molière put on plays there. Louis XV lent the château to his father-in-law Stanislas Leszczynski, the exiled king of Poland, and later gave it to Marshal de Saxe as a reward for his victory over the English and Dutch at Fontenoy in 1745. The marshal had a splendid time: not only wine, women and song, but also military exercises for his regiment of 1,000 foreign cavalry, which he watched from the roof; you can rent horses at the stables he put up on the grounds. After his death, the château was neglected, and the furniture was destroyed or disappeared in the Revolution. Then the duc de Bordeaux received it, becoming comte de Chambord; he later failed, through political stupidity, to become king of France. His collection of toy weapons can be seen upstairs; Henry James, who was here a year before the count's death, wondered "if he should take it into his head to fire off all his little cannon, how much harm the comte de Chambord would do." Apparently the bigger ones can pierce a stone wall.

All visitors owe a debt of gratitude to Canon Gilg, an elderly Alsatian who was parish priest of Chambord in August 1944. He succeeded in persuading the retreating Germans to give up their plan of destroying the château, together with the hostages imprisoned in it; a feat which would have eclipsed that of General Ludendorff, who—as readers of Barbara Tuchman's *A Distant Mirror* will remember—blew up the 700-year-old castle of Coucy in the previous war, just for fun.

Now the château and its forest belong to the state; vast rooms are open to the public, and have in the last few years been filled with exhibits. Not all of these concern Chambord, but they are interesting nonetheless.

The Château

Open daily except public holidays 9:30–11:45 and 2–4:30, 5:30 or 6:30, depending on the season; visitors can stay inside the building an extra 45 minutes. Guided tours in French and English, or wander freely with an excellent leaflet in English.

First, some figures: the facade is 420 feet long; there are 440 rooms and 365 chimneys; around the château are 13,000 acres of forest—the public has access to only 3,000 of these—surrounded by a wall 32 km. (20 miles) long.

Despite its grandeur, Chambord has drawn mixed reviews.

Chambord

"The most outstanding experience of the Loire valley," says one writer. "A huge, expensive folly," says another. "Megalomaniac," says a third, "an enormous film-set extravaganza." John Evelyn saw it in 1644; considering that 1,800 workmen were constantly employed in building it for 12 years, he complained —uniquely—that it was not big enough. Just before the Revolution, Arthur Young expressed puritanical disapproval, suggesting that the King should turn the rather spindly game forest over to intensive turnip cultivation. Henry James did not know quite what to think: "monstrous . . . the redundancy of its upper protuberances . . . an irresponsible labyrinth . . . " Still, he enjoyed his visit, especially his ramble—which modern tourists can repeat—along the roof-terrace among "the towers, the turrets, the cupolas, the gables, the chimneys [which] look more like the spires of a city than the salient points of a single building."

The visitor might start with the *diaporama,* a 15-minute audiovisual show about the castle in alternating French and English. This is one of those agreeable châteaux in which you can wander as you please without a guide. You will inevitably use the famous double spiral staircase; it looks like one staircase, but a regiment could march up one spiral while another descended the other without their meeting. At the very top, the roof terrace deserves Henry James's enthusiasm.

A good shop at the château exit sells not only postcards and books, but also super-8 films, video cassettes and cardboard models of Chambord and other châteaux to cut out and assemble.

Hotel

St.-Michel (M), Chambord (tel. 54–20–31–31). 38 rooms, some with bath or shower. Closed early Nov. to late Dec. Garage. Tennis. Good value for location; an ideal spot from which to tour the château. Restaurant. It has a convenient cafe terrace from which you can admire the château while slaking your thirst.

Restaurant

Le Relais (E), 1 av. Chambord, 41250 Bracieux (tel. 54–46–41–22). Closed mid-Dec. to late Jan., and Tues. evenings and Wed. Limited number of tables; book in advance. One of France's best restaurants, elegant and moderately expensive. M. Robin, owner and chef, is so good that critics even rave about his *potatoes.*

Those who do not want a gourmet lunch will find Bracieux a good place to buy picnic materials. Market is on Thursday mornings in a fine covered marketplace. Bracieux also has a few small restaurants, modest compared with the splendors of Le Relais.

Fast Facts

Tourist Office: Best information on the area from Blois tourist office.

Son et Lumière: In April and May, Fri., Sat., Sun. and public holidays; June through Sept. nightly. Starts between 9:30 and 10:45, depending on season. More detailed information from the château.

Châteauneuf-sur-Loire

Orientation

This riverfront town of 6,000 inhabitants 25 km. (15 miles) east of Orléans on N60 is a convenient base for explorations of nearby sights, including Saint-Benoît, Germigny-des-Prés, Sully, the Parc Floral at Olivet and even Orléans for those who prefer not to stay in big towns. It has its own attractions, too; not dramatic or stupendous ones, but certainly interesting and pleasurable. Despite a dull and traffic-laden main street, Châteauneuf is a gracious, leafy town, full of parkland and ideal for leisurely strolling; the tourist office has marked walks of up to five hours along the Loire and the surrounding countryside. The town is at its liveliest on Fridays, when the weekly market is held.

Sights

Château Park. The château no longer exists. There was a castle here in the 10th century which was wrecked in the Wars of Religion. In the 17th century, Louis Phélypeaux de la Vrillière, Louis XIV's Secretary of State, built a miniature Versailles on the site. That château was destroyed in the Revolution and its violent aftermath; all that survived were a few out-buildings. These —a pavilion, the orangery and some stables, among others— now form the town hall. They stand around a charming formal garden; there is a wide moat with terraces and flowerbeds at the bottom. There are fine views from this complex, which also includes an exhibition hall and the Musée de la Marine.

Below the formal gardens stretches a delightful park, laid out in the 1820s à l'Anglaise—not in geometrical forms but in a "natural" way—with giant tulip-trees from Virginia, 34 kinds of oak and vast numbers of rhododendrons, which flower in late May and early June. Chinese-looking streams snake their way to the Loire under magnolias and weeping willows; there are benches and picnic spots on the banks.

Eglise St.-Martial. Opposite the château gates, this long church was, like much of the town, badly damaged during the last war. Instead of rebuilding the collapsed nave, architects ingeniously turned it into an arcade. Inside, the tomb of la Vrillière, saved from destruction during the Revolution when hidden by a barricade of barrels, is a striking piece of Baroque theater. His life-size effigy is in dramatic prayer, an angel points towards

Heaven, while in contrast to la Vrillière's 17th-century aristocratic respectability, two grinning skeletons look on. This massive work was carved in Italy, by a pupil of Bernini, and
transported to Châteauneuf by sea and up the Loire.

Musée de la Marine. Open July and Aug. daily, except Tues.,
10–12 and 2–5:30; June and Sept. closed weekday mornings;
April and May closed weekdays. Other months by appoint-
ment, for groups only. Leaflet in English. Tel. 38–58–41–18.

Located in the Château Park, this museum, with its 5,000
miscellaneous exhibits, is a fascinating tribute to navigation on
the Loire. Transport and traffic on the Loire, once a way of life,
ended with the coming of the railways. Here are bits and pieces
of boats, as well as models; and paintings, photographs and
documents relating the boatman's life. There is a newly established Documentation Center attached to the museum; serious
students of Loire navigation can apply to consult its books and
documents, which are regularly being added to.

Hotels

La Capitainerie (I), Grande-Rue (tel. 38–58–42–16). 14 rooms
with bath or shower. Closed Feb. In the Château Park, the best
hotel in Châteauneuf. Restaurant (M) closed Mon. except in
high season.

Nouvel Hotel du Loiret (I), pl. A. Briand (tel. 38–58–42–28).
21 rooms, some with bath or shower. Hotel and restaurant
closed Jan. and Sun. evenings, but hotel open Sun. evenings
June to Sept. Across from park. Garage.

Fast Facts

Tourist Office: pl. A. Briand (tel. 38–58–44–79). Opposite
château gates. Open weekday afternoons, plus mornings in high
season.

Chaumont-sur-Loire

Orientation

The view of Chaumont from across the Loire is delightful. Still, unless this is the only Loire château you plan to visit, you may be content to skip the guided visit and settle for the view. There are better rooms to be seen on a guided walk around Amboise or a self-propelled ramble about Chenonceau. The château entrance is at the bottom of the hill, near the traffic lights. Allow a good ten minutes to toil up a steep and stony path, and up to half an hour in the courtyard while waiting for the next tour; lovely views will reward your patience.

Chaumont lies on the south bank of the Loire, across the river from Onzain, which is 17 km. (10 miles) from both Blois and Amboise on N152. Onzain has an excellent luxury hotel, and the village of Chaumont itself has a fine riverside campsite.

The Château

Open daily April through Sept., 9:30–11:45 and 2:15–5:45; Oct. through Mar. 9:45–12 and 2–4; stables remain open 30 minutes later and are closed on public holidays. Guided visit; leaflets in English. Allow 45 minutes, not including stables.

Henry James was right:

> The towers, the pinnacles, the fair front of the château, perched above its fringe of garden and the rusty roofs of the village and facing the afternoon sky, which is reflected in the great stream that sweeps below, all this makes a contribution to your happiest memories of Touraine.

He could not go inside.

This 15th-century château was given to Henri II's mistress, Diane de Poitiers, by his wife, Catherine de Médicis, when she ejected Diane from the more beautiful Chenonceau after Henri's death. It did not please Diane, who soon left. Benjamin Franklin often stayed here, advising the then-owner on investments in the New World. Franklin is best-known in France as the inventor of the lightning rod and bifocals; he is shown wearing a pair on the terracotta medallion which commemorates his association with Chaumont. The château was heavily restored and modernized, central heating and all, by a sugar magnate in the last century. It is now owned by the state.

The park is a pleasant place for a stroll and a look at the outside of the château. If you make it up there, you should not miss the stables; a guided visit is included in the château admission.

Chaumont

Chenonceau

Orientation

The château is Chenonceau, the village is Chenonceaux—a spelling peculiarity which defeats most French people. Yet, aside from its spelling, Chenonceau, unlike Chambord, has provoked no arguments. Everyone from Diane de Poitiers, Catherine de Médicis and Mary Stuart onwards has found it "the most delightful château of them all," "this lovely place," "the most exciting and the most romantic of all Loire châteaux," to quote just a few recent writers.

There is agreement, too, about the present administration. The château and grounds are privately owned by a chocolate manufacturer; his imagination, good taste and consideration of the visitor's convenience and pleasure give satisfaction not only to students of history, architecture and the fine arts, but also to those who simply want a happy day out. You could spend the better part of the day here, looking around the château, sitting in the gardens, having lunch, and then taking another look inside—all without leaving the grounds. And there is a *son et lumière.*

Chenonceau's only drawback is its popularity, but on most days it absorbs its crowds quite well. As the visit is not guided, you can skip a room full of, say, French schoolchildren, and return to it later. Morning opening time sees the smallest crowds.

There is a big parking lot by the ticket office at the gates of the park.

History and Highlights

A rich tax-farmer, Thomas Bohier, began the château in about 1520, and got himself heavily into debt in the process. His son inherited the debt and the château; his only way out of bankruptcy was to hand the place over to François I. Henri II gave it as a present to his mistress, Diane de Poitiers; his widow, Catherine de Médicis, took it back on his death. Catherine was far from being an admirable character, but she had good taste when it came to homes and gardens, planning the charming three-story extension that spans the river Cher. In the 18th century the château was owned by the Dupin family, who entertained many of the celebrities of the day there. Their son's

Chenonceau

tutor was Jean-Jacques Rousseau; he remarks on the excellent food at Chenonceau in his *Confessions*. At the Revolution, the château and its treasures were spared destruction because of the esteem in which Madame Dupin was held by her proletarian neighbors.

The Château

Open daily 9–4:30, 5, 6, 6:30 or 7, depending on season; closed 12–2 mid-Nov. to mid-Feb. Wander freely; leaflets in English. Tel. 47–23–90–07.

Chenonceau is a place of pleasure rather than a fortress; its architecture is civilized, peaceful and feminine. A wide avenue leads towards the château between lawns crowded with swans who have left the moat for a stroll. Before going inside, walk around to the right of the building and lean on the parapet for a view of the river gliding under the arches of the gallery, the formal French garden and the woods beyond.

Inside the château is a profusion of splendid ceilings; colossal fireplaces; authentic furniture and, of course, paintings, including work by Rubens, Corregio and Andrea del Sarto. The well-

known portrait of Louis XIV by Regnier, copies of which are in
so many other châteaux, is here. In François I's bedroom, an
interesting triptych depicts the *Three Graces*. The women who
modeled for the paintings, the Mailly-Nesle sisters, were all
mistresses of Louis XIV at different times. There is a picture of
Diane de Poitiers as the goddess Diana, and another Diana by
an unknown 18th-century artist, with the usual dog, bow and
arrows, and a hunting horn that looks like an 18th-century
telephone. Nattier's portrait of Madame Dupin is quiet and
charming.

There is a waxwork exhibition, **La Musée des Cires,** in one
of the outbuildings, showing four centuries of history.

Hotel

Le Bon Laboureur (M), Chenonceaux (tel. 47–23–90–02). 29
rooms with bath or shower. Closed mid-Dec. to mid-Feb., Tues.
and Wed. lunch. Henry James ate here a century ago: "We took
our way back to the Bon Laboureur . . . and even after we had
dined we were still content to sit awhile and exchange remarks
about the superior civilization of France. Where else, at a village
inn, would we have fared so well?" The Bon Laboureur still
encourages comfort and geniality, though it has come up in the
world. Premises have been enlarged and made luxurious. Fine
nouvelle cuisine in the restaurant.

There are cheaper hotels and restaurants in the village. Back
at the château, the self-service restaurant is adequate for a
modest meal.

Fast Facts

Son et Lumière: A *promenade spectacle* in the château's
illuminated gardens. Nightly mid-June to mid-Sept., at 10.

Cheverny

Orientation

The village is Cour-Cheverny, the château is Cheverny. Don't be discouraged by the adverse reports of those who saw the château a few years ago. In the '70s, for example, one writer called it a "worst buy"; for about twice the price of a visit to Chambord, he was shown a few beautiful rooms, thickly furnished with gorgeous things—but far too rapidly, and in a crowd. As the family were still living there, he was excluded from most of the building and the gardens. Others were just as disgruntled.

Things are different now. More well-furnished rooms have been opened to the public, who may visit them without a guide. A visit can now be confidently recommended, especially when combined with one to Beauregard, nine km. (five miles) northwest on D765, or to Fougères-sur-Bièvre, 12 km. (seven miles) southwest.

The Château

Open daily, mid-June to mid-Sept. 9–6:30; rest of year 9:30–12 and 2:30–5. Guided tour optional; leaflets in English. Allow one hour. Tel. 54–79–96–29.

Cheverny, built of that useful Touraine tufa which hardens and whitens with age, was completed in 1634. It is still owned by the same house-proud family that built it; they filled the château with splendid furniture and fashioned, over the centuries, one of the most glorious interiors on the Loire. The painted and gilded paneling on walls and ceilings is magnificent, particularly in the "King's Bedroom," which boasts a superb sculpted and gilded fireplace. The coffered ceiling painted by Mosnier (1600–1656), who had a hand in nearby Beauregard, depicts the story of Perseus and Andromeda. In small neighboring panels, *putti* play-act the goings-on. You can easily get enough of faded tapestries on the Loire, but those at Cheverny showing the labors of Hercules retain their original glorious colors.

In the gallery is a bronze of George Washington and a document signed by him. Louis XVI and Washington founded the Society of the Cincinnati, reserved for officers who fought in the American Revolution—including three of the present owner's ancestors. Nearby is the owner's family tree, 1490–1978.

Those interested in hunting (called "venery" on notices and

in the leaflet) will perhaps enjoy the Trophy Room, on whose walls and ceiling are the antlers of 2,000 stags killed in the local hunt since 1850. "Venery" still goes on, with costumes and hunting calls, though huntsmen are now rationed to 30 stags a year. In the kennels next door, dozens of hounds lounge about waiting for their next meal. Feeding times are given on a notice—*la soupe des chiens*—for the benefit of those who appreciate the spectacle.

The château gardens and park are off-limits to visitors. Still, there are three benches from which to admire, on the right day, the green grass, blue sky and white château. Unless you're taking part in a conference there, you won't be able to visit the Orangery, where the *Mona Lisa* and other masterpieces from national museums were hidden during the war.

Hotels and Restaurants

Les Trois Marchands (M), Cour-Cheverny (tel. 54–79–96–44). 39 rooms with bath or shower. Closed mid-Jan. through Feb., and Mon. except April through Sept. Restaurant.

St.-Hubert (M), Cour-Cheverny (tel. 54–79–96–60). 20 rooms with bath or shower. Closed Dec. to mid-Jan. and Tues. in off-season.

Those interested in a gourmet meal should consider visiting *Le Relais,* at Bracieux, nine km. (five miles) to the northeast.

Fast Facts

Son et Lumière: On hunting themes, a few evenings in July and Aug. Details from Blois tourist office or château.

Chinon

Orientation

Chinon is both a great fortress-castle—spectacular from a distance, bare and ruined inside—and a medieval town nestling below it. Overlooking the river Vienne, 16 km. (10 miles) upstream of the Loire, Chinon is a quick 48 km. (29 miles) southwest of Tours on D751, and 29 km. (18 miles) southeast of Saumur on D749. The town is convenient to other tourist attractions; Ussé is only 14 km. (eight miles) distant on pretty D16, while Azay-le-Rideau lies halfway between Chinon and Tours. There is a big free parking lot by D751 near the château.

There are a few trains daily from Tours, taking about 45 minutes and stopping at Azay-le-Rideau. Some of these take bicycles for free, and bicycles can be rented at Chinon station.

A word of warning: a ramble around the castle and down into the town involves a lot of walking on cobbled slopes. High-heeled shoes and open-work sandals will be a grave nuisance; "sensible" shoes or espadrilles, on sale cheaply everywhere, are recommended.

History and Highlights

The fortress dates from the time of Henry II of England, who also ruled most of France. He died here in 1189, and was buried a few miles away at Fontevraud. And here, two centuries later, occurred the famous scene of Joan of Arc's recognition of the disguised Charles VII. The fact that Joan was briefly at Chinon and that Rabelais (1494–1553) was born here has inspired street-namers, restaurant-owners and souvenir-sellers. They cash in, too, on the philosopher Descartes (1596–1650), who was born some 50 km. (30 miles) away. If the saintly warrior, the ribald novelist and the analytical thinker meet in a Chinon in Heaven, there is one thing they will agree upon: they are good for business down below.

The powerful and proud Cardinal Richelieu (1585–1642), Louis XIII's prime minister, owned the château, and used cartloads of its stones to build a new one at Richelieu, 24 km. (15 miles) away, leaving Chinon to fall into ruin. It is perhaps poetic justice that almost nothing remains of Richelieu's own château.

The Château

Open Feb. through Nov. daily, except Wed., 9–12 and 2–5 or 6; 9–6 June through Sept.; no Wed. closing mid-March through Sept. Guided visit. Tel. 47–93–13–45.

There is a walker's path from the parking lot on D751 to the château, a great ruined fortress with colossal walls, on a high spur above the river. It is worth paying the admission charge, if only to walk around behind the ramparts, admiring the views of town and river and reflecting on history. Amboise has similar views, but there the atmosphere is one of pomp and circum-

Chinon:
The clock tower

stance, art and elegance; here at Chinon, violence and the cruel hand of time.

All is open to the elements, except for part of the rebuilt *logis royaux,* the royal chambers, where there is a small museum. There is not much in it at present, besides a good genealogical

table of the kings of England and France and a model of the
château as it once was, but there are plans for extending it.

You can climb into the Coudray Tower, where the unfortu-
nate Knights Templar were imprisoned in 1302, leaving their
graffiti before being taken to Paris, tried and burnt. The Tour de
l'Horloge has a bell, named Marie Javelle, which has been
sounding the hours since 1399. Inside is a Joan of Arc Museum,
consisting mostly of pictures and French text; the tower itself is
worth the climb if you don't mind spiral staircases. Nearby is
a quarry from which came much of the stone to build this giant
fortress.

Other Sights

Vieux Chinon. Walkers can follow the signs marking the paths
and steps to the medieval part of town. The lazy way is to drive
down from the château parking lot; it's a shame to miss the
picturesque descent on foot, but there is much to be said for
avoiding the arduous climb back. The houses and narrow
streets below are charming; a particularly good walk can be
enjoyed by starting in pl. de l'Hôtel de Ville and wandering
down tiny rue Voltaire, once the town's main street.

A minor but amusing attraction of the town is its echo. Walking from the parking lot—the one by D751—to the castle, you
will see a small road marked "Echo" forking off to the right.
Two hundred yards down are steps at a vineyard gate; stand on
them and yell. The great castle walls face you, and will return
a sharp, clear response. Of course, if you shout anything ending
in the word "Chinon," you will be answered with a loud,
French *"Non!"* —a fact that has been taken advantage of for
centuries by local playboys requesting information about the
ladies of the town.

Musée du Vin. In the tourist office's vaulted cellars (tel. 47–93
–25–63). Open April through Sept. daily except Thurs., 10–12
and 2–6 or 7. English spoken; allow 30 minutes. A fascinating
museum, especially for those who know a little about vine-
growing, wine-making and barrel-making. Admission charge includes tastings of the local product, much of which is of superi-
or quality.

Musée Vieux Chinon. In the former Hall of the Estates-Gener-
al (tel. 47–93–18–12). Open daily except Tues; Feb. through
May and Sept. through Dec. 10–12 and 2–5; June through Aug.
10–12 and 3–7. Some fascinating exhibits in splendid rooms, all
relating to local history.

Château de la Grille. About one mile north of town on D16. Tel. 47–93–01–95. Loire wines are mostly white, but since long before the time of Rabelais—who was eloquent in their praise—fine red wines have been made in the Chinon-Bourgueil area. Among the best is Château de la Grille, about a mile north of town. If you're lucky, you will be shown around by Jean Manceau, the young and enthusiastic manager.

The vineyard is a small one: about 45 acres. The output is modest and depends on the weather—around 75,000 bottles a year, though in some years almost none is made—and is relatively expensive. The methods of production combine the most modern—computerization and stainless steel, among other things—with the most traditional. Wine is matured in small oak barrels for a year or two in cellars carved out of tufa, followed by further maturing in glass bottles stacked deep in a maze of tunnels.

Cheaper local wine is "Easter wine," bottled and sold the year after production, but the wine of this château improves with age and rivals the best Bordeaux. The 1982 vintage, delicious and perfumed already, will probably be even better in the year 2000. The bottles themselves are modern reproductions of a practical 18th-century shape; among the trimmed bushes in the front of the château is a big clipped living bottle. A few bottles of this wine, acknowledged to be among the best examples of what Chinon produces from the cabernet franc grape, will make suitable souvenirs for enjoyment back home.

Hotels

Château de Marçay (E), Marçay (tel. 47–93–03–47). 34 rooms and 3 suites, fully equipped. Closed mid-Jan. to mid-March. Seven km. (four miles) south of the city center on D749 and D116, this luxurious and peaceful château/hotel has a modern annex, an excellent restaurant, a swimming pool, gardens and tennis courts.

France (I), 47 pl. Général de Gaulle (tel. 47–93–33–91). 26 rooms with bath or shower. Open mid-March through Nov.; closed weekends except in high season. In the center of town. Garage, no restaurant.

The municipal **campsite** is across the bridge from Saumur on the south bank of the Vienne.

Restaurants

Au Plaisir Gourmand (M), 2 rue Parmentier (tel. 47–93–20–48). Closed two weeks in Nov., one week in Feb., Sun. evenings and Mon. The best restaurant in Chinon; elegant and refined. It is wise to reserve a table.

There is a good market on Thursdays in pl. de l'Hôtel de Ville. On the same street, the **Jeanne d'Arc,** a pizzeria well patronized by locals serves inexpensive wine by the jugful.

Fast Facts

Tourist Office: 12 rue Voltaire (tel. 47–93–17–85). From mid-June to mid-Sept. there is a branch in the parking lot next to the château.

Son et Lumière: Fri. and Sat. evenings in high season; details from tourist office.

Excursions: In July and Aug., there are day cruises on the Vienne and the Loire in 72-passenger boats, with visits to châteaux, wine-tastings, etc. Details from the tourist office or from Val de Loire Croisières, pl. de la Liberté, Thuré, 86140 Lencointre (tel. 49–93–98–46).

An ancient steam train, for tourists only, plies the rails between Chinon and Richelieu, hooting cheerfully, throughout the high season. The tourist office can give details.

Fontevraud

Orientation

This quiet town of 2,000 inhabitants 15 km. (10 miles) south-west of Saumur was home for centuries to an unusual religious community of nuns and monks. Its abbey church is central to the histories of both England and France. Today it houses a cultural center, with residential accommodations, an open-air theater and facilities for conferences, concerts and sports. Restoration—indeed, excavation—continues. More historical finds are made yearly, and there is work here for researchers which should last decades.

History and Highlights

The abbey was founded in 1099, and rapidly prospered. It soon comprised five communities—nuns, monks, lepers, repentant female sinners and the sick—each of which had its own church, cloisters, dormitory and kitchens. All five were controlled by a series of aristocratic abbesses who attracted generous donations and exercised influence in high places. The Plantagenets were great benefactors; many blue-blooded ladies joined the order, and others were educated here.

Between 1115 and the French Revolution in 1789, there were 39 abbesses. William the Conqueror's grand-daughter was one; five belonged to the royal House of Bourbon. The marquise de Montespan, Louis XIV's mistress (she had seven children by him), retired here; her sister, Gabrielle, was a celebrated abbess, under whose administration Fontevraud knew its greatest glories.

All this was swept away by the Revolution, and much of the complex was destroyed. In 1803 Napoleon converted the remaining buildings into a prison, and such it remained until 1963. Restoration, much of it carried out heavy-handedly by convict labor, began in the last century.

The Abbey Church

Open daily, except Tues., April through Sept. 9–12 and 2–6:30; Oct. through March 10–12 and 2–4. Guided visit only; leaflets in English. Tel. 41–51–71–41.

The guided tour begins at the abbey church itself. Until recently, it housed convicts in several stories, but all the cells and staircases have been removed. Once more, this great 12th-century church, bare and austere, roofed with a series of domes, offers the imaginative visitor a lesson in building vast structures in stone. This is the burial ground of the Plantagenets: Henry II of England, who ruled from Scotland to the Pyrenees; his wife Eleanor of Aquitaine; their son Richard Coeur de Lion; and their daughter-in-law Isabelle of Angoulême, widow of (bad) King John. Their bones were scattered at the Revolution, but are probably somewhere in the crypt; excavation is continuing. The crowned and sceptered effigies from their tombs—three in stone, one in wood—are in a remarkable state of preservation and have retained their original colors. In the 19th century Napoleon III agreed to have them removed to England, but a wave of protest kept them where they are, which is where Henry and his relations wished to be.

The Gothic and Renaissance Sainte-Marie Cloisters lead to the Renaissance chapter house. Here are the emblems of François I and the Bourbons on paving stones, as well as 16th-century paintings of religious subjects featuring prominent abbesses and friends of the abbey. These underwent occasional changes, one face being replaced by another when gratitude or flattery dictated.

Next to the long vaulted refectory, now used for concerts, is an extraordinary eight-sided kitchen. Its tall pyramidal spire is in fact one of the abbey's 20 chimneys, which rise skywards in a bizarre marriage of the sacred and the practical. Some of its eccentricity is the result of over-zealous restoration in 1902; photographs of its earlier state are on display. Just outside the entrance, the Church of Saint-Michel has some fine works of art rescued from the abbey.

New discoveries and improvements in conditions and displays can be expected over the next few years. At present the abbey is a unique spectacle, somewhat spoiled by impatient guides wielding keys.

Hotel

La Croix Blanche (I), 7 pl. des Plantagenêts (tel. 41–51–71–11). 19 rooms, some with bath or shower. Closed last two weeks in Nov. A good, simple hotel. Restaurant offers rock-bottom prices and cheery service, as well as more elaborate fare.

Abbey of Fontevraud

Restaurants

La Licorne (M), rue d'Arbrissel (tel. 41–51–72–49). Closed two weeks from late May, one month from early Dec., Mon, Tues. lunch. In a fine old house near the abbey. *A la carte* only; asparagus in puff-pastry with tarragon-flavored butter recommended. Tempting dessert trolley.

L'Auberge de l'Abbaye (I), tel. 41–51–71–04. Closed part of Oct., part of Feb., Tues., Wed. lunch except in high season. The solid menus cooked by M. Côme win high praise from locals.

Fougères-sur-Bièvre

Orientation

The château at Fougères-sur-Bièvre is an excellent example of fortress architecture. It is relatively small, and has no furnishings or works of art inside, but a stop here is recommended, especially as a short detour from more famous places in the area. Cheverny, Chaumont and Beauregard are within 15 km. (10 miles), and Amboise and Blois are about twice that distance.

Fougères is a tiny and charming village. The "sur-Bièvre" part of its name distinguishes it from the considerable town in Normandy, which also has a château. With luck there will be few other visitors when you arrive; there's always parking space in front of the château. Across from the château is one of those nice little village cafés where an able Frenchwoman dispenses drinks, sells newspapers and cigarettes and fills drivers' tanks from the pump outside.

The Château

Open April through Sept. daily except Tues., 9–11:45 and 2–6:30; Oct. through March daily except Tues. and Wed., 10–11:45 and 2–4. Guided visit; leaflet in English. Allow 30 minutes. Tel. 54–46–27–18.

Pierre de Refuge began building the present château in 1470, after the original fortress on the site had been wrecked in the Hundred Years' War. Instead of following fashion and building an elegant Renaissance structure, he built another fortress, dourly defensive, with slits instead of wide windows, and machicolations—for dropping stones and boiling oil on attackers—around the tops of the walls. It exudes even today the spirit of the Middle Ages, although a 16th-century owner put in "modern" windows here and there, and the moat and drawbridge have since been done away with.

The caretaker, who serves as guide, lives with his wife in a pretty cottage inside the gates, by the stream which flows under the château; this stream powered a small textile factory inside during the last century. The outside of the château is worth a few minutes' inspection while you wait for a tour.

The tour, recommended only for those strong of wind and limb, involves clambering up below the extraordinary carpentry of the roof and along the *chemin de ronde,* looking down through the machicolations, and whizzing up and down spiral staircases. Although there is nothing to steal and little that visitors could damage, the tour is guided for reasons of safety, and the guide is always shouting *"Attention à la marche! Attention à la tête!"* (Mind the step! Watch your head!)

Fougères
The gallery

Germigny-des-Prés

Orientation

This village of 400 inhabitants, famous for its ancient church, is situated on the north bank of the Loire five km. (three miles) southeast of Châteauneuf-sur-Loire and the same distance northwest of St.-Benoit, which, with its famous abbey, is well-combined with Germigny-des-Prés on a daytrip.

The Church

Open daily 9–7, until 8 in summer. Very small, Germigny-des-Prés is often called the oldest church in France. Perhaps, in its own strange way, it is the most beautiful. To say that it is a square, pre-Romanesque or Byzantine arrangement of rounded arches on square pillars, with indirect light filtering from smaller arches above the central square, is to give an inadequate idea of the quiet beauty of the place. It makes an unforgettable impression on most visitors, even if they spend only five minutes here.

The church was built in about the year 810 by Theodulf, an abbot of St.-Benoit. It fell into a ruinous state (the Vikings again), though it was patched up enough to serve as the village church in the 13th century. In the middle of the last century it was energetically restored; indeed, rebuilt. What we see today could be described as a modern replica—with an added nave—of the church as it was over a thousand years ago. Whatever people think of this sort of restoration in general, most are grateful in this instance.

Mosaics, dating from the year 500 or earlier, were brought by Theodulf from Ravenna in Italy to decorate the church. Most of them were destroyed, but one, covered by a layer of plaster, was discovered by children in 1848. Composed of 130,000 cubes of colored glass, it shows the Ark of the Covenant escorted by two angels with golden halos. Charlemagne, who often visited Theodulf, saw this Byzantine mosaic. In the Latin inscription around the edge, Theodulf asks us not to forget him in our prayers. Later additions to the church include some interesting statuettes in wood dating from the 15th to 17th centuries.

One often has the Germigny church to oneself. Postcards, booklets, and leaflets in English are laid out on a table.

Gué-Péan

Orientation

Gué-Péan is neither a state museum nor a showpiece designed to process thousands of visitors a day; it is the home of the marquis de Keguelin, whose family, or remote branches of it, have lived here for centuries. Though roads to the château are well-marked, it takes some effort to find, as it nestles in a wooded valley, down country lanes a mile or so from the village of Monthou-sur-Cher, 10 km. (six miles) from Montrichard.

Like many aristocrats, the marquis cannot afford to keep the building in good repair without letting the public in; rather than install a fun-fair on his 6,000 acres, he and his small staff take in paying guests as well as daytime visitors. "Each admission charge," says the marquis, "pays for a new slate on the roof."

History and Highlights

This moated château dates mainly from the 16th century. Louis XII, Henri II and François I slept in the Chambre du Roi; so, more recently, did the late Shah of Iran. There is a tenuous connection with English history—it was probably here that the aged Louis XII's wife and Henry VIII's sister, Mary of York, met the handsome Charles Brandon, duke of Suffolk. When she became a widow she secretly married Suffolk, against Henry's orders but with François I's connivance. Henry eventually forgave them and they lived out their lives happily in England. They were the grandparents of the ill-fated Lady Jane Grey.

The Château

Open daily for visits; mid-March to mid-Oct., 9–7; Jan. to mid-March, 10–1; mid-Oct. through Dec. 10–5. Guided visit; English-speaking guides. Allow 45 minutes. Tel. 54–71–43–01 and 54–71–46–09.

Gué-Péan is a fascinating place, even for those who come only for the guided tour of part of the premises. This is a family home, and while it would not be fair to call the contents a muddle, they are certainly a surprising and very human miscellany.

Visitors first see the chapel, where members of the family have been married since 1672, and where there is a memorial

le Gué Péan

to Resistance fighters killed in the last war. The marquis was in the Resistance from 1940; he is a Compagnon de la Libération, and took a leading part in the insurrection in Paris in 1944, just before General Leclerc's troops arrived.

Next is the dining room, where lucky paying guests will dine with the marquis later in the evening. Here are Beauvais and Aubusson tapestries, Louis XVI furniture, portraits and a curious 18th-century painting thought to be an advertisement for a society midwife: a very pregnant but cheerful lady is combing her hair and having something complicated explained to her by an efficient-looking companion.

There is plenty to admire in the Chambre du Roi, the King's Bedroom, and in the drawing rooms, including porcelain and pictures of Chopin and George Sand, who were friends of the marquis's great-aunt. Other curiosities include royalist banners, Sicilian puppets, family souvenirs and an elegant traveling bidet for an elegant traveling lady.

Some visitors will find it hard to leave the library, where, under glass, are autograph letters—mostly written to the marquis or his ancestors—from Louis XVI, Napoleon and de Gaulle, and especially from writers, including Victor Hugo, Marcel

Proust and Jean-Paul Sartre. A certificate signed by the governor of Wisconsin proclaims August 9, 1983 marquis de Keguelin Day.

Staying at the Château

For the price of a relatively expensive hotel room, a couple can share the room in the Great Tower. There are other rooms, some cheaper, depending on size and the value of the furniture. Dinner can be provided, with good wines, at moderate prices. The marquis says:

> The food I am able to serve is not *haute cuisine,* yet no one has been poisoned so far. The plumbing occasionally sounds like a medieval siege, but when all is said and done my guests are in touch with the France they came to see. Not a plastic, sanitized-for-their-personal-protection France, but a living and breathing country proud of its ancestry.

Langeais

Orientation

Langeais is not among the half-dozen "top" châteaux of the Loire, but it is certainly an important one for students of architecture and furniture. Still, there are drawbacks to Langeais. The little town, on the north bank of the Loire 25 km. (15 miles) downstream of Tours, is on the way to or from a number of other important châteaux and towns, including Saumur, Fontevraud, Chinon, Azay-le-Rideau and Villandry. Its narrow streets are often crowded with traffic; many tour-bus operators include it in their tours so as to cram one more château into the itinerary. Rows of buses wait to enter the parking lot and disgorge throngs of tourists. Don't be surprised if, after reaching the parking lot and crossing to the château, you find yourself in the middle of a crowd. Architectural features, fireplaces and furniture similar to those of Langeais are to be seen in other châteaux on the Loire, in conditions of less hardship. So if you are in this part of the Loire simply for pleasure, you could well skip Langeais—or stop for a moment, pop into the entrance lobby and buy some postcards, just to prove you've been there. Having warned pleasure-seekers that less joy can normally be expected here than at other places within a short distance, it is fair to say that some visitors speak highly of Langeais.

The Château

Open daily except Mon. mid-March through Sept., 9–12 and 2–6:30 (no lunchtime closing July and Aug.); Oct. to mid-March 9–12 and 2–5:30. Guided visits only.

Langeais was built, but not completed—there are only two wings of the four planned—from 1465 to 1469 on the orders of Louis XI. His aim was to ward off Breton incursions into the Loire valley from Nantes. Soon afterwards, his successor Charles VIII married Anne of Brittany in the château itself, uniting Brittany with France and removing the menace.

The last private owner filled the château with a notable collection of tapestries, pictures and furniture, and left it all to the state in 1904. A visit gives a respectable sample of fortress architecture, including a good *chemin de ronde* above the machicolations. Superb fireplaces, tapestries, beds and chests offer insights into Renaissance life.

Langeais

Visits are strictly supervised. In each room, a bored guide points to various objects described on a tape recording. Leaflets in several languages are *lent*. The effect is not very pleasing.

Hotel

Le Langeais (M), 2 rue Gambetta (tel. 47–96–82–12). 12 rooms, some with bath. Closed three weeks from late June, three weeks in Jan. and Mon. evenings and Tues. With excellent restaurant—chef Jean-Jacques Hosten wins loud praises for his ways with fish, and for his duck with orange.

Le Lude

Orientation

Le Lude itself is rather out of the way, on the Loir (*not* the Loire) 48 km. (29 miles) northeast of Saumur and 50 km. (30 miles) northwest of Tours. When approaching it by car, do not be misled by signposts to Château-du-Loire, which is a neighboring town and not the château you are looking for.

The Château

Open daily April through Sept., 3–6 (gardens only, 9–12). *Son et lumière* after dark Fri. and Sat. mid-June to early Sept., and a few other days in July and Aug. Full details and seat reservations from main tourist offices (Angers, Saumur, Tours, Blois, etc.) and from local tourist office.

The château itself is in a mixture of styles, built over the centuries. The interior contains some interesting furniture and

le Lude

tapestries, but most visitors will have seen finer sights along the Loire (*not* the Loir). Le Lude is included in this book only for its magnificent *son-et-lumière* spectacle, enlivened by fireworks and fountains, with over 300 costumed performers in a pageant of the history of the château and the region from the Hundred Years' War to the end of the 19th century. Bus companies provide excursions to performances from most of the larger places further south.

Hotel

Hotel Maine (I), 24 av. de Saumur (tel. 43–94–60–54). 24 rooms with bath or shower. Closed part of Sept., Dec. and Jan. Restaurant (closed Mon.). Garage.

Fast Facts

Tourist Office: Summer: pl. de Nicolay; winter: 8 rue du Boeuf (tel. 43–94–62–20).

Loches

Orientation

Despite gloomy tales of Louis XI's dungeons, a fine morning or afternoon at Loches should provide some of the pleasantest memories of a stay in the Loire. All the more so if you pass up the most direct route by car and pick your way through delightful wandering country roads among green fields, rivers, streams and woods. Loches is 41 km. (24 miles) southeast of Tours on N143, but only the most hurried should fail to leave that road at Corméry, taking D17 along the banks of the Indre and rejoining N143 at Chambourg-sur-Indre. From Chambourg, it's better to cross the Indre and make a detour in the Forest of Loches, where the Plantagenet kings hunted deer.

Coming from Montrichard or Chenonceaux, one can take in Montpoupon and, with a detour, Montrésor, 25 km. (15 miles) from Loches on the pleasant D760, on which you pass the great gateway of the Chartreuse du Liget. This was a monastery founded by Henry II of England in expiation for the murder of Thomas Becket; it was remodeled in the 18th century and then abandoned at the Revolution.

Like Chinon, Loches is a walled citadel dominating a small medieval town. Both are awe-inspiring from a distance. Chinon's citadel, when one reaches it, is a rather sad, ruined shell, but the citadel of Loches is in an excellent state of preservation in parts, is much bigger, holds many items of interest, and is a living part of its town.

You can drive up and park in rue de la Poterie, by Porte Royale, the entrance to the citadel. But there is also a big parking lot by the railway station convenient to N143 and D760, and only ten minutes' walk through the narrow pedestrians-only streets to the citadel.

As for trains, little has changed since Henry James came by rail from Tours, complaining of the awkwardness of the timetable; he did not get long enough at Loches. The return journey can still be done; inspect the timetable carefully, noting which trains run on which days. If you are staying at Loches, the trains allow a long day to be spent at Tours, starting early in the morning. Bicycles may be hired at Loches station.

The Château

Open daily Feb. through Nov., except Tues., 9–6; 9–12 and 2–5 or 6 other months. *Donjon* open same hours as château except they are 30 minutes later. Ticket needed for the *Logis Royaux* (the château itself) and the *donjon* (the fortress keep); bought at the château, it covers both guided visits. Allow 40 minutes for the *Logis Royaux,* 50 minutes for the *donjon.*

Henry James was peeved at Loches; the administrative offices of the sub-prefect were in the château, and that worthy had the exclusive use of terraces, obviously commanding magnificent views but off-limits to visitors. Fortunately the *sous-prefecture* was moved elsewhere in 1925, and we can enjoy the gardens from which James was excluded. In his time there was "a horse-chestnut tree of fabulous size, a tree of circumference so vast and perfect that the whole population of Loches might sit in concentric rows beneath its boughs." Alas, in 1950 it was struck by lightning and had to be cut down.

You can stroll outside on the terrace of the château and gaze over the river and roofs below, and at the château's pointed towers and swallows' nests. Inside, lectures on French history—in French, though leaflet in English—may go on too long for many tastes, especially as one may well have heard much of it before in other châteaux. There is a good copy of Fouquet's well-known portrait of Charles VII looking sour, and a horribly efficient-looking two-man crossbow, with multiple pulleys, capable of piercing a thick door at 200 yards. And then there is Agnes Sorel, Charles VII's mistress, exposing a shapely breast, surrounded by blue and red angels and looking as though butter would not melt in her mouth, for Fouquet was painting the Virgin and Child; and her tomb, with lovely, smiling Agnes in alabaster upon it, and lambs—a play on her name: *agneaux* is the French for lambs—at her feet. She died in 1450 at the age of 28; rumor had it that she was poisoned at the instigation of Charles's son, the future Louis XI, while Charles, 20 years after Joan of Arc had done her work and perished in the flames, was driving the last of the English from France.

There is an interesting triptych of the Crucifixion by the school of Fouquet, with all the participants in 15th-century costume. There is also an exquisite little chapel which Charles VIII built for his queen, Anne of Brittany, with hundreds of sculpted ermine tails, Anne's emblem.

You can walk as your own master to the fortress towers—*le donjon.* The word is usually translated on leaflets as "dungeon," which is wrong, although the towers do contain dungeons, *cachots* in French. One ruined tower, the *donjon* itself, can be inspected without the guide. This rectangular 11th-century keep is now roofless, but brave spirits can climb up the steps inside. The other towers, built later, may be seen with the guide. These should please everyone who enjoys seeing prison cells and torture chambers, and hearing about the hardships Louis XI inflicted upon those who met with his disapproval.

Leave the citadel at the foot of Martelet Tower, with its cells for important prisoners like Ludovico Sforza, duke of Milan, who fell foul of a kindlier king, Louis XII, the "people's friend." An easy and picturesque half-hour's walk will take you back to the station parking lot: turn left and follow the path in the moat until you reach rue Quintefol; then immediately climb up again, below the church of St.-Ours, and follow the narrow rue St.-

Loches: Tomb of Agnès Sorel

Ours towards the Cordeliers' Gate. If you have left your car in rue de la Poterie, you'll have to thread through the pedestrian streets for nearly an hour.

Other Sights

Eglise St.-Ours. There's no need for a ticket to see much of the citadel; the walled city on its hill is part of the town, and one of the first bits of it you're likely to see is the church of St.-Ours, with its striking roof of eight-sided pyramids. These date from the 12th century; the remainder of the church was finished by the 15th century. There is an amazing sculptured doorway in the porch: acrobats, monkeys, mythical beasts, owls and funny faces. These, unlike the sadly damaged Virgin above them, have come unscathed through France's religious troubles. Inside is a font converted from a pagan Roman altar, as well as a touching epitaph to the *vénérable et discrète personne,* priest of this church, who had been a chaplain to the French prisoners of war in England during the Napoleonic wars.

There are two minor museums in the citadel. The **Musée Lansyer** was the home of the 19th-century landscape painter of the same name, and contains many of his paintings. The nearby **Musée du Terroir,** inside Porte Royale, concentrates on local history. Open daily except Fri., 9–11:45 and 2–4; until 5 in Mar., Oct.; until 6 Easter through Sept. One ticket covers both guided visits; allow 45 minutes.

Hotel

George Sand (I), 39 rue Quintefol (tel. 47–59–39–74). 17 rooms with bath or shower. Pleasant, inexpensive and on the river. Meals on the terrace in good weather.

Fast Facts

Tourist Office: pl. de la Marne, near the railway station (tel. 47–59–07–98). Open July to mid-Sept. Organizes 90-minute evening walks around the old town. English-speaking guides.
Son et Lumière: Many evenings June to Aug. Details at main tourist office.

Meung

Orientation

Meung is a pleasant town of 5,700 inhabitants near an exit of the A10 highway 18 km. (11 miles) southwest of Orléans. Situated on the north bank of the Loire, with a bridge to the south bank, it is strategically placed for either a visit en route to somewhere else, or a stay at its riverside campsite or in one of the dozen rooms at the inexpensive Auberge St.-Jacques.

History and Highlights

Meung has its place in literary and military history. Its most famous citizen was Jean de Meung. Born about 1260, he wrote the greater part of *Le Roman de la Rose,* a best-seller for centuries which Chaucer translated into English. François Villon, poet and criminal, was imprisoned at the château until Louis XI passed through Meung in 1462 during his coronation celebrations and pardoned him. The château was also headquarters for Lord Salisbury, who commanded the British troops at the siege of Orléans in 1429, until he was killed by a cannonball. His replacement, Talbot, could not prevent Joan of Arc's victory at Orléans. Her troops went on to capture the château, which became headquarters for her and the duc de Alençon for two months before they marched north to defeat the English at Patay.

From the 12th century until the Revolution, the château was normally the residence of the bishops of Orléans, as well as being a prison under their administration. It suffered in the 16th-century religious troubles and was sold off after the Revolution. It was empty, dilapidated and closed to the public at the time it was bought by its present British owner, Mr. Tachon, in 1970.

The Château

Open daily May to 11 Nov., 8:30–5; rest of year Sat., Sun. and public holidays only, 9–5. Allow one hour for guided visit. English-speaking guide; leaflets in English. Tel. 38–44–36–47 and 38–44–25–61.

The château is an odd mixture: part 12th-century fortress, part 18th-century residence. Mr. Tachon has furnished the château with his own collection—everything from French 12th-century to English Chippendale to souvenirs he has picked up during his long career (a Channel Islander living in France, he escaped from the Germans and worked for the Allies' Underground in World War II). In one room are weapons from crossbows to Bren guns, and helmets from the Middle Ages to 1939–45.

The most memorable part of the château is below ground level, where Mr. Tachon is actively engaged in exploring and reopening an extensive network of subterranean cells, storehouses and corridors. There is said to be a flooded medieval tunnel from the château all the way to Cléry St.-André on the other side of the Loire. Highlights of the guided visit, sometimes led by Mr. Tachon himself, include an underground chapel, torture chambers and secret tunnels. Touring visitors will get plenty of exercise between the château's cellars and its two acres of roof.

Hotel

Auberge St.-Jacques (I), rue Général de Gaulle (tel. 38–44–30 –39). 12 rooms, some with bath. Closed Mon., and for two weeks in both mid-Oct. and late Jan. Fine restaurant. Garage.

The café opposite the château gates is pleasant and inexpensive for lunch.

Fast Facts

Tourist Office: 42 rue J. de Meung (tel. 38–44–32–28).

Montbazon

Orientation

Apart from a ruined 12th-century keep with an enormous 19th-century Virgin perched on top of it—and two minutes' gaze is enough for that—tiny Montbazon presents nothing extraordinary. Likewise, the traffic on the busy main road to Poitiers does not add to its meager attractions. But readers with enough money will find many excellent luxury hotels nearby; and Montbazon is convenient to the major sights of the region.

It lies a mere five km. (three miles) from the A10 (Paris–Bordeaux) highway, a couple of hours' glide from the capital. A dash on the motorway takes you to Blois, whence smaller roads lead to Chambord, Cheverny and lesser places. The center of Tours is 13 km. (eight miles) from Montbazon, Amboise 34 km. (20 miles), Chenonceaux 31 km. (18 miles), Loches 32 km. (19 miles), Azay-le-Rideau 22 km. (13 miles), and Villandry, by zigzag lanes, about 22 km. (13 miles).

Hotels

Le Château d'Artigny (E, very). Tel. 47–26–24–24. 48 rooms, 7 suites. Closed Dec. to mid-Jan. In a 60-acre park two km. (one mile) north on D17, this is one of France's best hotels. It was built at the turn of the century by Coty, the perfume tycoon, in pseudo-Louis-XV style, and has everything that can be expected of a very expensive palace-type hotel. Its restaurant (especially the desserts) and wine cellar are justly famous. Le Relais, at Bracieux, rates slightly higher among connoisseurs (restaurant only, no rooms) but the d'Artigny is close on its heels.

La Domaine de la Tortinière (E). Tel. 47–26–00–19. 14 rooms, 7 suites. Closed mid-Nov. through Feb. (restaurant closed Mon. and Tues. lunch in March and from mid-Oct.). Two km. (one mile) north on N10 and D287, La Domaine, in a big park sloping down to the river Indre, is preferred by some because it is smaller, as châteaux go, and more intimate. There is a bedroom with a round bed and a TV in the ceiling for those who prefer that sort of thing. Swimming pool and tennis.

Le Moulin Fleuri (I). Tel. 47–26–01–12. 10 rooms with shower. Closed last two weeks Oct., first three weeks Feb. and Mon. except public holidays. Five km. (three miles) outside of town, with a pleasant terrace on the banks of the Indre.

Restaurant

La Chancelière (M), 1 pl. des Marronnieres (tel. 47–26–00–67). Closed three weeks in Nov., 10 days in July and Sun. evenings and Mon. except public holidays. A charming vine-clad spot with fine *foie gras* and salmon dishes *à la carte*. Low-priced lunch *menu* on weekdays.

Fast Facts

Tourist Office: At the Mairie. Tel. 47–26–03–31.

Montgeoffroy

Orientation

If you are traveling between Saumur and Angers on the picturesque south bank of the Loire, this minor but rewarding château is a ten-minute drive north from the bridge at St.-Rémy-la-Varenne. A visit can be combined with an excursion to Plessis-Bourré, 35 km. (21 miles) to the northwest.

The Château

Open daily April through Oct., 9:30–12 and 2:30–6:30. Allow 45 minutes for guided tour. Leaflets in English. Tel. 41–80–60–02.

There is nothing warlike about Montgeoffroy. It is a graceful château meant to be lived in—and it has been lived in, and lovingly cared for, by the same family ever since the marshal de Contades built, furnished and decorated it in the 1770s. The elegant, white facade is as it always was; so is most of the interior, giving an intimate glimpse of aristocratic French life before the Revolution.

There is a noble view from the gates of the château, surrounded by its French gardens. Enter along the wide driveway, and park beside the château. Some timid souls park outside the gates, but the gravel of the drive is hard on unsuitably shod ladies.

Everything inside is in excellent condition: furniture; paintings, including some good family portraits; and *objets d'art.* Signed photographs of the Queen Mother and Prince Charles give a more recent touch; they were visitors, too.

There is an elegant chapel with interesting ceiling bosses. In the stables, horse-drawn carriages are on show. Noteworthy is a 19th-century English stage-coach which used to ply the Nice–Cannes route. Horsey people will love the circular saddling room, with its smell of polished leather and its collection of equipment from the past.

Montpoupon

Orientation

Montpoupon is about 15 km. (nine miles) south of Chenonceaux and the same distance south of Montrichard en route
from either to Loches. Loches is 20 km. (12 miles) south of
Montpoupon; if you are going there, consider stopping at this
minor château. You need not necessarily venture inside.

The Château

Open mid-June through Sept. 10–12 and 2–7 (no midday closing Sat., Sun. and public holidays); other months open afternoons on Sat., Sun. and public holidays; closed Nov. through
Feb. English leaflets. Allow 35 minutes for guided tour. Hunting
museum open varying hours mid-March through Sept. Tel. 47–
94–23–62 and 47–94–30–77.

Montpoupon, still inhabited, is mainly a 15th-century château, with some 13th-century features, among them its towers.
The guided visit offers little to non-specialists who have visited
other châteaux, besides another lecture in French.

La Musée de la Vénerie (Museum of Hunting), within the
château, will appeal to those interested in fox and stag hunting.
Its exhibits include trophies and hunting equipment from years
gone by, and recordings of hunting horns. The château also
boasts an ancient kitchen, in use up until 1975.

Montrésor

Orientation

Montrésor lies 27 km. (16 miles) south of Montrichard by picturesque little roads, and 25 km. (15 miles) east of Loches; it makes a convenient detour between the two towns. The château is a minor one, and doesn't figure prominently on many tourist itineraries. This can be a blessing; if you're lucky, you might have the guided visit all to yourself.

The Château

Open daily April through Oct. 9–12:30 and 2–6. Guided visits only; in French, with explanations in English. Tel. 47–94–20–04.

Montrésor was started as a fortress in the 11th century; from the ramparts that remain is a pleasant view over the village, with the little river Indrois snaking away among meadows. It was rebuilt in the 16th century by Imbert de Bastarny, a prominent local whose tomb in the village churchyard is worth a visit.

Montrésor

In the 1850s, Montrésor was bought and remodeled by Count Branicki, a Polish emigré who went with Napoleon III to Constantinople during the Crimean War and became a French senator. The château has been kept much as he left it; it's largely a typical mid-Victorian gentleman's home crammed with souvenirs of Poland's tragic history. Those who know a bit about Poland and the Victorian era will find Montrésor instructive and moving; those who don't may consider it a bit of a bore.

One of the highlights of the interior is a spiral staircase transported from the 1889 Paris Exhibition. But there's also plenty of hunting and shooting paraphernalia. There are acres of oil paintings: one fine Italian primitive depicts *The Crossing of the Red Sea,* in which the sea is the size of a small river but *very* red. There are several portraits, several of the family, one by "dear old Winterhalter," as Queen Victoria called him. Other full-length portraits are only copies, but copies of originals destroyed at the Russian Revolution. A colossal canvas in the billiards room describes the Polish Revolt of 1861.

Many items in the château relate to the Polish hero, King John Sobieski III (1629–1696), who helped defeat the Turks and free Vienna; these include gorgeous silver and gold vessels presented to him by the Viennese. In the garden is a touching statue, cast in 1861, of the death of Polish officer Count Kaminski, who served in the French army and was killed at the battle of Magenta.

Château guides here can be somewhat elusive. If no one comes when you ring the bell at the entrance, walk down rue Potocki for a look at the church before trying again.

Montreuil-Bellay

Orientation

Montreuil-Bellay is a small town dominated by its château, in a pleasant site with public gardens along the river Thouet. The river joins the Loire at Saumur, 18 km. (11 miles) north on N147.

The Château

Open daily, except Tues., April through Oct., 10–11:30 and 2–5:30. English-language tape recordings on guided visit; allow 45 mins.

The 15th-century château is colossally picturesque from the outside, with pointed roofs sticking up from its defensive towers. Inside, there are good tapestries and furniture, a chapel with frescoes of angelic musicians, vaulted cellars, and one of those staircases people used to go up on horseback, just to show off. The superb medieval kitchen is reminiscent of Fontevraud, but with some 19th-century equipment.

Montreuil-Bellay

Hotels and Restaurants

Hotel Splendid and **Relais du Bellay** (I), rue Dr. Gaudriez (tel. 41–52–30–21). Under one management; between them 41 rooms, many with shower or bath. Closed last two weeks in Jan. and Sun. evenings mid-Sept. to Easter. The Splendid has a restaurant, the du Bellay a heated pool.

Restaurant La Porte Saint-Jean (I), 432 rue Nationale (tel. 41–52–30–41). Closed Feb. and Mon. evenings and Tues. Inexpensive local traditional cooking and Saumur wines.

Fast Facts

Tourist Office: pl. des Ormeaux (tel. 41–52–32–39). Open mid-June to mid-Sept.

Montrichard

Orientation

Montrichard has no remarkable "sights," but it rates an honorable mention as a pretty town of 4,000 on the banks of the Cher. It has good hotels and is admirably situated in the heart of an area where sights are thick on the ground. Within a half-hour's drive are Amboise, Blois, Chaumont, Chenonceaux, Loches and Tours; a little further are Azay-le-Rideau, Chambord and Villandry. Many lesser but interesting places, including Beauregard, Fougères and Gué-Péan, are within a short distance. Montrichard therefore makes a good base for those who want neither the big-city attractions of Tours nor the touristic bustle of Amboise or Blois.

The Château

The keep (*le donjon*) and museum open daily mid-June to early Sept., 9:30–12 and 2:30–6:30; other months Sat., Sun. and public holidays. Closed Oct. to late March.

Most of Montrichard's château is in ruins, due to various troubles between 1188, when Richard Coeur de Lion was besieged in it, and 1940, when the Germans set up their artillery in it and were shelled by the French from across the river. But visitors can still climb to the top of the square keep for splendid views, and there is a modest museum of local antiquities in its ticket office.

Hotels

Château de la Menaudière (M–E), postal address 41400 Chissay-en-Touraine (tel. 54–32–02–44). 25 rooms, fully equipped. Open mid-March through Nov. Closed Sun. evenings and Mon. except May to mid-Oct. A real château, built in 1443 at the same time as Chenonceau, peacefully hidden in a park two km. (one mile) outside Montrichard on the road to Amboise. Totally renovated and modernized. There is a sharp, modern bar in the turreted gatehouse, and the food in the elegant dining rooms is entirely satisfactory.

Bellevue (M), quai du Cher (tel. 54–32–06–17). 29 rooms, most with bath or shower. Closed mid-Nov. to late Dec., and Mon. evenings and Tues. from Oct. through April. On the river with good views. Restaurant.

La Croix Blanche (I), 62 rue Nationale (tel. 54–32–00–43). 14 rooms, some with bath or shower. Closed Feb. Excellent value for rooms and food.

Tête Noire (I), 24 rue de Tours (tel. 54–32–05–55). 39 rooms, most with bath or shower. Closed early Jan. to early Feb., and Fri. from mid-Oct. to mid-March. Good restaurant.

Restaurant

Le Grill du Passeur (I), 2 rue du Bout-du-Pont (tel. 54–32–06–80). Closed Dec. to mid-March. A modest local eating place in a 15th-century house on a bridge over the Cher. Specialties include grilled eels and skewered duck hearts, as well as good plain steaks.

Fast Facts

Tourist Office: At the Mairie (tel. 54–32–00–46).

Montsoreau

Orientation

Visitors to Fontevrauld will almost certainly pass through Montsoreau, a charming village on the Loire five km. (three miles) north of Fontevrauld on D147. Even those staying at Saumur, 11 km. (seven miles) west on D947, should spend a morning taking in the facade of Montsoreau and the splendid view downstream from its terrace.

The Château

Open daily, except Tues., April through Sept. 9–12 and 2–7; rest of year, 9–12 and 2–5. Guided visit; allow one hour.

An interesting story has this château as its setting. The lady of the château was having an affair with Bussy d'Amboise. When her husband found out, he forced her to have a rendezvous with the lover at another château, where Bussy was murdered. Back at Montsoreau, husband and wife—and this is the moral of the story—let bygones be bygones, and lived happily for 40 years, producing nine children.

The château's military facade is 15th-century, and access is through an old tunnel under a house. Its interior is given over to the **Musée des Goums,** a collection of exhibits transferred from Morocco in 1956. The museum is concerned primarily with Marshal Lyautey's conquest of that country, and with the Goums, Moroccan soldiers who fought under the French flag in both world wars.

A ten minute walk uphill brings you to the famous view, or *belvédère*—a long stretch of the Loire, with the Chinon nuclear power station looming in the distance. Also marked is the road to a windmill, the **Moulin de la Herpinière;** in the mill itself and in adjoining cave-rooms, its artist-owner exhibits some of his sculpture, paintings, tapestries and furniture.

Hotel

Bussy et Diane de Méridor (I), tel. 41–51–70–18. Closed mid-Dec. through Jan. and Tues. except evenings in July and Aug. Some of the 19 rooms look out over the château, as do the terraced gardens on the hillside. The restaurant has a good cellar of Loire wines.

Onzain

Orientation

Like Montbazon and Montrichard, Onzain figures in this guide not for any on-the-spot sights, but because it is a pleasant town conveniently situated for seeing major châteaux and places of interest. It offers hotels at all levels of price and comfort, as well as a campsite.

Onzain lies opposite Chaumont on the north bank of the Loire, 16 km. (10 miles) upstream of Blois, 20 km. (12 miles) downstream of Amboise and 44 km. (26 miles) downstream of Tours. Chenonceaux, Cheverny and Chambord are within 40 minutes' easy driving. A good route between Tours and Onzain, for those willing to go slowly and stop and stare, is the little road that runs below the hills along the riverbank, parallel to the much busier N152. It goes via Vouvray, Nazelles and Cangey, where the fields are white with ducks whose day-old offspring are sent all over France. Good wine can be bought from producers along this road, and you can gaze your fill at horses, cows, sheep, goats and half-hidden mini-châteaux.

Onzain is on the main railway line that goes along the Loire, but only a few Paris trains stop at its little station. Careful study of the timetable can allow train-users to visit Tours, Amboise, Blois, Beaugency, Meung and Orléans, although it would be more practical to stay at Tours or Blois, and get off the train for a day at Onzain. Bicycles can be hired at the station and left elsewhere. Henry James "did" Chaumont from Tours, getting off at Onzain, and the thing he liked best about Chaumont was the view of it from the bridge as he went back to Onzain station.

Hotels and Restaurants

Domaine des Hauts de Loire (E), route d'Herbault (tel. 54–20 –72–57). 22 rooms, 6 suites. Open mid-March through Nov. A luxury château-hotel three km. (two miles) out of Onzain, in the same category as the Château d'Artigny at Montbazon. In a vast park, it offers everything (except a swimming pool) one could expect from its high prices, including delicate inventive cooking in surroundings of appropriate elegance.

Château des Tertres (M), route de Monteaux (tel. 54–20–83– 88). 14 rooms, all with bath. Open week before Easter to early Nov. Breakfast, but no restaurant. One mile out of town, this is really a *gentilhommière*—a 19th-century gentleman's country house—rather than a château. In a 12-acre park with good views over the river to Chaumont. English spoken.

Pont d'Ouchet (I), 50 Grande-Rue (tel. 54–20–70–33). 10 rooms. Closed Dec. through Feb., Sun. evenings and Mon. Simple but gratifyingly inexpensive. It is doubtful whether anyone does *moules marinière* better than Monsieur Cochet, and his profiteroles (with ice cream inside and hot chocolate sauce over) would not disgrace a more luxurious restaurant. Madame Cochet's advise on wine can be relied upon.

The *cave coopérative* at Onzain should not be missed by wine-lovers. Here, some of the best wines of this fortunate Touraine region are sold, and may be sampled.

Orléans

Orientation

Of the three important towns in the region covered by this guide—the others are Tours and Angers—Orléans seems the least loved. Certainly Tours offers more attractions and is a better base for excursions. On a rapid tour of the Loire valley, Orléans may reasonably be omitted. But it is a city worth getting acquainted with.

An hour's train ride from Paris and just 130 km. (78 miles) away on the A10 highway, Orléans is easily visited. Highways bypass the town, freeing its streets from much through traffic. Visitors coming from Paris without cars can easily spend a day and a night in Orléans, rent a car the next day to see nearby places, and return to Paris that evening. Using similar tactics, longer excursions from Paris could include Tours and its great neighboring châteaux.

Many visitors to Orléans prefer to stay in the suburb of Olivet four km. (two miles) south of the Loire. Olivet is almost like a small country town, with its own little river, the Loiret. Here are plenty of hotels and restaurants, as well as the Parc Floral de la Source, one of Orléans's great attractions.

History and Highlights

Orléans has always been in the thick of French history, and has seen its share of glory and suffering. The Loire is a natural barrier; Orléans is a strategic bridgehead at the center of France. Julius Caesar found its inhabitants a nuisance; he slaughtered them and burnt the town. Five centuries later, Attila arrived with his Huns and more fire and sword. Childeric and his Franks disputed the town with Odoacer and his Saxons, and the Normans, of course, did some pillaging and sacking of their own. Under the Valois kings, Orléans became a secondary capital. The story of Joan of Arc and the Siege of Orléans during the Hundred Years' War cannot, alas, be retold here. In the Wars of Religion, the greater part of the cathedral was destroyed by the Huguenots. In the Franco-Prussian War of the 1870s, Orléans suffered heavily. The Germans destroyed half the town in 1940; the Allies sent their bombers in 1944. A self-inflicted wound was the destruction of many fine buildings by energetic town planners a century ago. Town planners are still at work

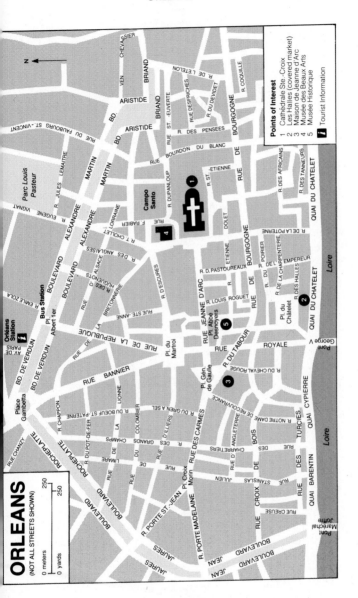

ORLEANS
(NOT ALL STREETS SHOWN)

0 meters 250
0 yards 250

Points of Interest

1 Cathédrale Ste.-Croix
2 Les Halles (covered market)
3 Maison de Jeanne d'Arc
4 Musée des Beaux Arts
5 Musée Historique

ℹ️ Tourist Information

today, modifying parts of the city with greater sensibility and
success; and Orléans is beginning to be loved again.

Sights

Cathédrale Ste.-Croix. Open daily, closed noon–2. The cathedral is a short walk from the theater; there is an underground
parking lot nearby, below Campo Santo, once a cemetery.
Coming from the railway station, cross the wide boulevard
Alexandre Martin and head down rue de la République, a
crowded main shopping street. This leads through the main
square, place du Martroi, and into rue Royale, with more good
shops; the Chocolaterie Royale will bring cries of ecstasy from
all but dieters. A left turn into rue Jeanne d'Arc brings you to the
cathedral.

The cathedral evokes mixed feelings; Marcel Proust called it
France's ugliest church. Well, like Mount Everest, it is certainly
there, and spectacular, a riot of pinnacles and gargoyles. After
its destruction by the Protestants, building in the Gothic (or
pseudo-Gothic) style went on through the 17th, 18th and 19th
centuries. The wedding-cake towers are 18th-century. You
have to be a very difficult person—and Proust could be *difficile*
—not to enjoy gazing at the outside from various viewpoints,
even if you don't feel you should wholly approve.

The majestic interior's great rose windows carry the sun motif
of Louis XIV. Other stained-glass windows—uninspired, but big,
19th-century work—tell the story of Joan of Arc. She does of
course have her chapel here, with a 20th-century monument;
before the altar kneels a statue of Cardinal-Bishop Touchet of
Orléans, whose tireless efforts led to Joan's canonization in
1920. Beside her chapel are two plaques, in memory of the
million British Empire dead of World War I, most of whom lie
in France, and of the half-million American dead of the two
World Wars. In the choir, the beautiful 18th-century wood-
carving should not be missed.

Musée des Beaux-Arts, 1 rue Ferdinand Rabier, next to the
cathedral. Open daily except Tues. 10–12 or 1 and 2–6. This
modern building features pictures by Le Nain, Boucher, Nattier,
Watteau, Courbet, Boudin and Gauguin, among the French
artists; and Tintoretto, Corregio and Velásquez, among the "for-
eigners." Sculpture, too: Rodin, Maillol, Zadkine and Gaudier-
Brzeska, who spent most of his short life in England but was a
native of Orléans. This is one of those easy galleries where you
take an elevator to the top floor and work your way down-
wards. Those who have read his poems will be touched by the

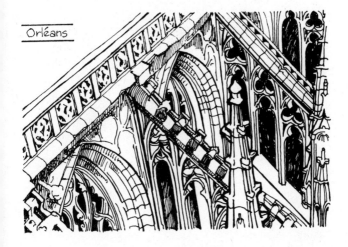

Orléans

cheerful watercolors of Max Jacob, who lived at Saint-Benoît, near Orléans, until 1944, when at age 68 he was dragged away by the Gestapo to die in prison.

Musée Historique, in the Hôtel Cabu, pl. Abbé Desnoyers. Open daily except Tues., 10–12 and 2–5 or 6. Admission charge, but free Sun. mornings and Wed. This is not a hotel, but an elegant Renaissance townhouse, with works of art both "fine" and "popular" illustrating the history and traditions of Orléans. They include a remarkable collection of pagan bronzes of animals and dancers found in a sandpit near Saint-Benoît in 1861. They had been hidden there, probably in the 4th century, during the anti-pagan activities of St. Martin of Tours.

Maison Jeanne d'Arc, pl. du Général de Gaulle, down rue Tabour, on the other side of rue Royale. Open daily except Mon. May through Oct. 10–12 and 2–6; other months 2–6 only. Joan stayed on the site, in a fine big house, which later underwent many changes before being bombed flat in 1940. It's no secret that the present house is a mere post-War reconstruction of the original, with exhibits about Joan, contemporary costumes and models of siege engines.

Parc Floral de la Source, eight km. (five miles) south of Orléans in Olivet (tel. 38–63–33–17). Open daily April to 11 Nov., 9–6; rest of year, 2–5. Admission 5 frs., reduced for shorter hours; accompanied children free. This is a rather special park. For one thing, the river Loiret bubbles up here, and immediately forms a respectable river in the middle of the park; it emerged all at once in 1672. Research has shown that the water comes from the Loire some 42 km. (25 miles) upstream from Orléans. As it passes underground, it warms up slightly, so that it is always comfortably above freezing. Flamingos, ducks, black and white swans disport themselves on the green. There are mighty trees and a mini-zoo, with deer, emus, parrots and peacocks, swings and picnic places, a tramway for when your feet get tired and a passable restaurant.

But the flowers are the thing. The Parc Floral serves as a showcase for nurserymen and seedsmen of the region. There are acres of flowerbeds, all clearly labeled. Avid gardeners should take a notebook; it will be difficult to drag them away. There is an information kiosk, for expert advise; at the entrance to the park one gets a useful plan of the layout. Come in April or May for 100,000 flowering bulbs and 70,000 spring plants, in May for azaleas and rhododendrons or in June for the iris show. From mid-May to June, 100,000 rosebushes bloom, and there is a rose show with prizes.

Other Sights

Other places of interest in Orléans include the fine shops on rue Royale and the **Nouvelles Halles,** the big covered market off rue Royale at the river end. The tourist office can sometimes arrange visits to the **Bollée Bell Foundry,** still producing big church bells in a suburb of the town.

Hotels

Auberge de la Montespan (E), 31 av. Georges-Clemenceau, St.-Jean-de-la-Ruelle (tel. 38–88–12–07). Two km. (just over a mile) out of town on the Blois road. 10 rooms with bath or shower. An old hunting lodge in an attractive garden sloping down to the Loire. Pleasantly relaxed, old fashioned ambiance and furnishings, plus excellent classical cuisine.
Sofitel (E), 44 quai Barentin (tel. 38–62–17–39). 108 rooms. Swimming pool. TV in most bedrooms. Restaurant La Vénerie (M) attached.
Frantel La Reine Blanche (M), 643 rue Reine-Blanche, Olivet (tel. 38–66–40–51). 65 rooms, fully equipped. Swimming, tennis, views of the Loiret and Orléans cathedral. Good, inexpensive restaurant; closed Sat. lunch.
Le Rivage (I rooms, M–E meals), 635 rue Reine-Blanche, Olivet (tel. 38–66–02–93). 21 rooms with bath or shower. Closed Feb. Restaurant is the best in Olivet; delicious food on a waterside terrace.

Restaurants

La Crémaillère (M *menus,* E *à la carte*), 34 rue Nôtre-Dame
de Recouvrance (tel. 38–53–49–17). Closed four weeks from
late July, Sun. evenings and Mon. Best in town for a gourmet
meal.
Le Lautrec (M), 26 pl. du Châtelet (tel. 38–54–09–54). Closed
last two weeks Feb., last two weeks July, Sun. Wine by the glass
and excellent advice from the *patron* on Loire wines.

Fast Facts

Tourist Office: pl. Albert ler (tel. 38–53–05–95). Out of season
open Mon. to Sat. 9–12 and 2–7; in season Mon. to Sat. 9–
12:15 and 2–7:30, Sun. 9:30–12:30; July and Aug. Mon. to Sat.
9–7:30, Sun. 9:30–12:30 and 3–6. Full service, including hotel
reservations anywhere in France, guided tours (groups by ap-
pointment, individuals Wed. and Sat. afternoons). Near the theater, with plenty of parking space. Due to move into new
premises by the train station in 1988.
Festivals: *Fête de Jeanne d'Arc:* the May 8th thanksgiving
festivities which Joan of Arc launched in 1430 get bigger and
better every year. Processions, with the "Joan" of the year
leading them on her white war-horse, flags and bands are still
to be seen on the 8th and days leading up to it. More information at the tourist office.
Car Hire: *Avis,* 13 rue de Sansonnieres (tel. 33–62–27–04);
Hertz, 47 av. de Paris (tel. 33–62–60–60); *Europcar,* 81 rue
Andre Dessaux (tel. 33–73–00–40).

Plessis-Bourré

Orientation

Plessis-Bourré should not be confused with the nearby Plessis-Macé or with Plessis, near Tours, both of which are far less interesting. The château is some 20 km. (12 miles) north of Angers by N162 and D768. A good visit could include driving along the Loire east of Angers to take in Montgeoffroy, and then going in an arc via Seiches, Tiercé and Cheffes; or after a drive in the Corniche Angevine west of Angers, going in an arc via St.-Georges-sur-Loire, Bécon and Grez-Neuville.

The Château

Open daily July and Aug., 10–12 and 2–7; closed mid-Nov. to mid-Dec.; rest of year open daily, except Wed. and Thurs. morning, 10–12 and 2–5. Guided visit; leaflets in English. Tel. 41–32–06–01.

Jean Bourré profited from being one of Louis XI's top civil servants. His château was built in its entirety between 1468 and 1473. From the outside, it seems a traditional fortress, on a courtyard plan with round corner towers, *chemin de ronde,* machicolations and—since the château is not on a defensible height—a great moat, almost a lake, crossed by a bridge nearly 50 yards long. In the courtyard, the Renaissance makes itself felt; this is a place for comfortable and dignified living, rather than for dour battles and bitter sieges.

Much of the interior resembles those of more important—and crowded—châteaux: tapestries; excellent collections of 15th- and 18th-century furniture; a chapel; a room where justice was administered, with a small prison opening off it; the library in a long gallery, with a collection of fans in glass cases; and the Grand Salon, a big, bright room with wide windows penetrating the thick walls and giving onto the moat and its waterlilies.

What makes Plessis-Bourré special is the ceiling of the Salle des Gardes, which is divided into 24 hexagonal panels, each containing very curious paintings. Jean Bourré was something of a chemist, which in the 15th century also meant something of an alchemist (the castle prison seems to have doubled as a laboratory). Most of the paintings in the Salle des Gardes have to do with occult aspects of 15th-century chemistry, although some merely illustrate folk tales or proverbs. Perhaps, taken altogether in some particular order, they convey a coded mes-

le Plessis-Bourré

sage about the elixir of life or the philosopher's stone; perhaps Bourré commissioned them just for fun. In some respects they suggest the dream world of the paintings of Hieronymus Bosch. There is a topless lady steering a land-yacht with wooden wheels, thought to be an allegory of spirit (the wind) and matter (the vehicle). There are people ceremoniously passing water, thought to be a reference to the fact that ammonia can be extracted from urine. In one of the frames, a she-wolf of dubious ancestry is taking a bite out of a startled lady. The wolf is thin, its sole diet being faithful wives, a commodity in short supply. The decorations between the panels must surely have been painted for fun; one of the dogs is straight out of James Thurber.

The only way to have anything like enough time for this unique ceiling is to gaze upward and pay absolutely no attention to the guide as he gives his lecture on the furniture. Photography is strictly forbidden. Perhaps someday an enterprising publisher will commission a coffee-table book with a page for each panel and specialist notes. Until then, interested visitors will go away tantalized.

Hotel

Château de Tieldras (E), Cheffes, 49330 Châteauneuf-Sur-Sarthe (tel. 41–42–61–08). 11 rooms, fully equipped. About five km. (three miles) from the château, this 16th-century country house in a 60-acre park is owned by the Count and Countess de Bernard du Briel. Excellent rooms, fishing, helipad. Restaurant top-notch (closed Tues. lunch); superb selection of Anjou wines.

Saché

Orientation

In the Middle Ages there was a castle here, but what is now called the château is actually a comfortable country house, partly 16th-century, partly 18th, with lawns and trees and a pleasant view over a valley.

None of this sounds particularly exciting. But visitors who have enjoyed reading Balzac and can follow spoken French will find a visit here an unforgettable experience. Those who don't care for Balzac and understand no French may find Saché a waste of time. Saché is seven km. (four miles) southeast of Azay-le-Rideau on D17, and convenient to Villaines-les-Rochers, Chinon, Langeais and Villandry.

The Château

Open Feb. through Nov. 9–12 and 2–5 or 6; closed Wed. except mid-March through Sept. Guided visit; leaflets in English. Tel. 47–26–86–50.

From time to time in his agitated life, but mainly in the 1830s, Balzac took refuge in Saché. Sometimes he was hiding from his creditors, sometimes just needing peace and quiet; always he pursued his prodigious creative life, rising in the small hours and sitting at his desk (it is still here), working 12, 14, 16 hours a day, sustained by cup after cup of coffee (and here is the pot) and in the evenings reading aloud his day's production to his friends. These were the Marjonnes, who owned the house. They, and it, and the countryside around figure prominently in his novels.

The house has been kept as it was in Balzac's time. Exhibits connected with his life and work have been added, including a fine collection of pictures of Balzac, Madame Hanska and people and places connected with them. A look at the proof-corrections on display will bear witness to his passion and dedication. Balzac had to pay, as authors still do, for corrections and additions beyond a certain limit. Painfully in debt, he made emendations filling all the margins of his proofs, causing dismay to his printers. Their legitimate bills for extra payment meant that some of his books, best-sellers for a century-and-a-half, failed to bring him a centime.

Saché benefits from an admirable guide who is, as we go to press, one of the château's main assets. She is a small, middle-aged lady who radiates enthusiasm, loves Balzac, knows all

about the house and seems very happy in her work. After her
guided visit, you'll understand why people claim Touraine
French is the best and clearest in France. Most visitors leave
Saché sharing her enthusiasm and determined to read a lot
more Balzac.

In the village square is one of the "stabiles" of Alexander
Calder, the 20th-century American sculptor, who settled in
Saché.

Restaurant

Auberge du XIIe Siècle (M), tel. 47–26–86–58. Modern food
in a genuine medieval setting.

Saint-Benoît

Orientation

St.-Benoît was St. Benedict, founder of the Benedictine order of monks. One comes to this tiny village 10 km. (six miles) southeast of Châteauneuf-sur-Loire to see the great abbey church, referred to on village signposts as *la Basilique*.

History and Highlights

St. Benedict died in the year 547. In his monastery at Monte Cassino in Italy, he had established a "rule" followed today in over a thousand monasteries worldwide. About the year 650, Benedictine monks chose this hill, safely above a fertile but often flooded valley, to be the site of a new monastery, which they called "Fleury." According to Julius Caesar, it had long been a Druidic holy place. Soon, the monks sent a delegation— a raiding party, according to some—to the temporarily abandoned Monte Cassino, and returned with the bones of St. Benedict, giving his name to their abbey. Some of the remains were sent back to Monte Cassino when monastic life re-started there; a certain amount of controversy has occurred.

The monastery has had its ups and downs. At its best, in its earliest days, it was a center of learning, sending monks to England and elsewhere to organize studies. Vikings and Normans vandalized the library and did their usual pillaging. It fell into decline after the Hundred Years' War under a series of absentee abbots appointed by the crown not for their piety but as a reward for services rendered. The Wars of Religion wrought grave damage; precious manuscripts were sold or burnt. At the Revolution the conventual buildings were destroyed and the monks scattered. The abbey church was fortunately saved; it became the parish church. It was not until 1944 that monastic life began anew here, with the monks rebuilding their monastery and regaining the abbey church.

The Abbey Church

Always open. Sung mass 11:45 weekdays, 10:45 Sun. and feast days. Vespers 6:15 daily. English leaflets; guided visits in English or French on written application to *Le frère responsable des visites de la Basilique* (tel. 38–35–72–43).

The present abbey church dates from the 11th century. Its

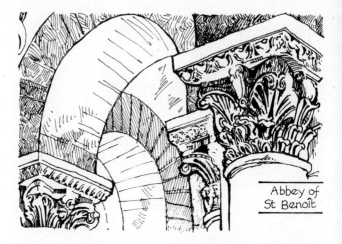

Abbey of
St Benoît

tower porch has remarkable carvings on the capitals of its pillars, some naively amusing, others touching. Inside is the crypt,
where St. Benedict's remains are kept in a chest. The great choir
and nave date from the same period. The choir has a delightful
patchwork floor of many-colored marble dating from the 4th
century; it was brought here from Italy to decorate the original
church.

   Gregorian chants can be heard daily, at mass or vespers. The
services on Sundays and feast days attract worshippers from all
around. When no service is in progress, visitors are welcome to
wander around inside and in the crypt. There is plenty of parking space outside, in the square under the lime trees.

Hotel

Le Labrador (I), tel. 38–35–74–38. 22 rooms with shower or
bath. Closed Jan. to mid-Feb. and Sun. nights Oct. to Easter.
Breakfast, but no restaurant.

Saumur

Orientation

This town of 34,000 inhabitants is one of the prettiest touring centers on the Loire. About 300 km. (180 miles) from Paris via Tours and A10, it makes an ideal base for exploring the western and central reaches of the Loire valley. Visitors are made welcome here. Saumur's château is impressive, its museums unusual. The country surrounding Saumur is a maze of tunnels and caves cut into cliffs, many of them full of sparkling wines and mushrooms; and pretty villages make superb excursions.

Fairly frequent trains between Tours and Angers stop at Saumur. The station is on the "wrong," northeast, bank of the river, about a mile from the château and tourist office.

History and Highlights

Now a fairly quiet provincial place, Saumur has memories of greater days. It was once an important center of Protestantism, with an academy and freedom of worship guaranteed to the Huguenots under Henri IV's Edict of Nantes. When Louis XIV revoked the Edict in 1685, the result for Saumur was crippling emigration. Indeed, it is only recently that the population has again reached its pre-1685 level. Railways killed the busy port, from which Anjou wines had been shipped downriver to the sea at Nantes, on their way abroad; today there is much more industry in the bigger neighboring towns of Angers and Tours. But Louis XVI did the town a good turn when he established the famous cavalry school here, which—after switching its course of instruction from horses to tanks—is still of considerable importance.

The Saumur cavalry cadets earned glory in 1940. Ignoring orders from the Pétain administration to withdraw safely to the deep south, and armed with only a few out-of-date practice weapons, its 1,200 men and 800 boys held out for three days on a 25-mile-long river front between Monsoreau and Gennes, keeping a vastly superior German force at bay. The colonel in charge was harshly criticized for this seemingly futile stand, which ended only when all the ammunition had gone and many cadets had died. Today, "the Cadets of Saumur" symbolize honor and courage.

The Château

Open daily July through Sept., 9–6:30 and 8:30–10:30; rest of year, 9 or 9:30–5 or 6; closed Tues. Nov. through March. Guided visit; leaflets in English. Tel. 41–51–30–46.

This white 14th-century castle towers above town and river. Once its roofs were a forest of pinnacles, and in that form it is seen in the frequently reproduced illumination from the *Très Riches Heures* of the duc de Berry. There were once dozens of windmills where today's parking lot and picnic areas are. All those excrescences have gone, but the château is still beautiful, worth going to even if you can spend only a few minutes in Saumur.

The castle is bright, cheerful and well looked after, from the fairy-tale gateway to the pots of fresh flowers here and there. There are two wonderful specialist museums in the château, and the only visitors who leave them displeased are those who feel they've been rushed through by the obligatory guide.

The **Musée des Arts Decoratifs** has good furniture, tapestries and wooden statuettes, but its highlight is a superb collection of china and porcelain, left to the city by a kindly connoisseur in 1919. The **Musée de Cheval** deals with horses, and is one of the highlights of a city no horse-lover should miss. In the museum are skeletons of prehistoric little horses and prize-winning big ones, as well as saddles and other equipment from Arabia, Texas and other wild places.

Yes, it's a pity you can't see the château at your own speed, but they are sensitive about theft here. The great key of the castle, which hung by the door, was carried off in 1918 by an American soldier. Fifty years later, his conscience troubled him. He returned it in person at a good-humored ceremony. The repentant thief was forgiven, speeches were made, and the Saumur wine flowed freely. But you cannot see the key today; it was stolen again a few years ago.

After the guided tour, you can get exercise and a fine view by climbing the spiral staircase of the watch tower, the Tour du Guet.

Other Sights

Ecole Nationale d'Equitation. Just outside town; visits by arrangement with the tourist office. This civilian institution, housed in highly automated and functional buildings, trains France's riding instructors and Olympic competitors, and is the home of the famous Cadre Noir team, so called because of their black uniforms.

Saumur:
Our Lady of Nantilly

Maison du Vin de Saumur, 25 rue Beaurepaire, next door to the tourist office. Open Mon. to Sat. 9–12:30 and 2–6:30. This museum has some good displays and offers helpful advice on visits to local producers.

Musée de la Cavalerie. In the Armored Warfare School Head-quarters, av. Foch. Open daily 9–12 and 2–5; closed Aug. Exhibits show the history of the Cavalry school from the 18th century to the present, with swords, uniforms and other para-phernalia.

Musée des Blindés, pl. du Chardonnet. Open daily 9–12 and 2–6. This museum houses 150 tanks and armored vehicles from 1918 onwards: early French models, German Panzers, Soviet T34s, American and British models and an odd motorbike on caterpillar tracks.

Vieille Ville. The streets between the château and the river are crammed with picturesque houses and churches. The area is particularly lively on Saturdays, when there is a good local market in pl. St.-Pierre. The tourist office arranges guided tours of the quarter at various times.

Excursions

A trip downstream as far as Gennes, 15 km. (10 miles) away, can be a charming one, with many temptations en route:

St.-Hilaire-St.-Florent. This suburb abuts a hillside pocked with passages and caves. Here, producers of sparkling Saumur wine—made the same way as champagne—are happy to show visitors around, tell them all about the virtues of this excellent product and give them a refreshing glass. The Saumur district also produces vast quantities of horse dung and mushrooms. It all fits: good tufa stone for building châteaux and houses can be cut out of the hillside in such a way as to leave damp, dark galleries; it is said there are 300 miles of them. Then, with a regular supply of horse dung and a few generations' accumulated skill, you are in business as a wholesale mushroom grower.

Musée du Champignon. Just outside St.-Hilaire. Open daily mid-March to mid-Nov., 10–12 and 2–6. Guided visit; leaflets in English. Allow an hour. Here you are taken on a subterranean stroll to learn all about the mushroom trade, and to admire some big fossils en route. The museum is the work of a private enthusiast, Monsieur Bouchard, who is usually there inspiring visitors with appreciation of the virtues of edible fungi. A fascinating tour, not to be missed.

Gennes. In this pleasant little river town, you can admire the view from the ruined church, and pay your respects at the graves of several of the Cadets of Saumur who were killed there. Once a busy port, the adjacent village of Cunault is famous for its own quite magnificent church, finished at the beginning of the 13th century. It has a wonderfully proportioned interior, with hundreds of carvings on the capitals of its columns, and interesting wood carvings.

Heading upstream the main excursion is to:

Caves Gratien et Meyer, just outside Saumur on D947 (tel. 41–51–01–54). Visits daily 9–11:30 and 2:30–5:30. Gratien and Meyer makes its sparkling wines in an underground city quarried out of the tufa cliffs, and offers perhaps the best wine visit in the district, with a film, a tour and a tasting.

Hotels

Le Prieuré (E), Chênehutte-les-Tuffeaux, 49350 Gennes (tel. 41–50–15–31). 38 rooms, fully equipped. Closed early Jan. to early March. In a 60-acre park eight km. (five miles) northwest of Saumur, this Renaissance manor house has been thoroughly modernized, with tennis courts, swimming pool and big windows overlooking the Loire. Its expensive restaurant is justly famed, particularly for its imaginatively prepared fish, excellent desserts and wine list. The best bedrooms are in the main building; the chalets in the gardens are unattractive from the outside but luxurious within.

Anne d'Anjou (M), 32 quai Mayaud (tel. 41–67–30–30). 38 rooms with bath or shower. Closed late Dec. to early Jan. 18th-century townhouse with views of river or château. No restaurant.

Campanile (I), Bagneux (tel. 41–50–14–40). 43 rooms with bath. A mile south of town on N147. Very modern.

Aux Naulets d'Anjou (I), rue Croix-de-Mission, 49350 Gennes (tel. 41–51–81–88). 20 rooms with bath. Restaurant. Open April through Nov.; closed Mon. except hotel in high season.

Roi René (I), 94 av. Général-de-Gaulle (tel. 41–67–45–30). 28 rooms with bath or shower. Restaurant closed late Dec. to early Jan.; Sat. lunch; and Sun. evenings and all day Sat. in winter.

There is a good **campsite** on the island opposite Saumur.

Restaurants

L'Escargot (M), 30 rue Maréchal Leclerc. Closed Nov., mid-Feb. to mid-March; Tues. evenings and Wed. Oct through April. A trustworthy local favorite.

Gambetta (M), 12 rue Gambetta. Closed Sun. evenings and Mon. Good local fare.

Fast Facts

Tourist Office: 25 rue Beaurepaire (tel. 41–51–03–06). Open mid-June to mid-Sept. Mon. to Sat. 9:15–7, Sun. 10:30–12:30 and 3–7; rest of year Mon. to Sat. 9:15–12:30 and 4–6.

Festivals: Every July, the cavalry school and the riding school present a big military tattoo—three days of horsemanship and displays by tanks and helicopters. Details at the tourist office.

Sully

Orientation

This town of 6,000 is the farthest point upstream this book covers. It's worth visiting if you're staying in the Orléans–Châteauneuf area or touring Saint-Benoît eight km. (five miles) away. But apart from the château, the 16th-century Church of St.-Ythier and the spire of another church, the rest of which is in ruins, there is little of architectural or tourist interest here. The center of town was destroyed by German shells in 1940, and Flying Fortresses finished the job in 1944.

The Château

Open daily, 9 or 10–12 and 2–5 or 6, depending on season. Guided tour; leaflet in English. Allow 50 minutes.

The château's most important owner was Maximilien de Béthune, duc de Sully (1559–1641). A Protestant—this is why his statue in the château shows him with a Bible—he was Henri IV's right-hand man, a statesman and economist of genius as well as

Sully

132

a notable soldier. He improved and enlarged what had been a 14th-century fortress, and laid out the pleasant park which lies across the moat. Strolling about the park, admiring the outside of the château and watching the anglers, is a good way to begin a tour of Sully.

The interior of the château has no objects of immense interest to those who have already toured several. It has, however, the biggest and best example of a chestnut roof anywhere on the Loire, a vast structure in the form of an upturned boat dating from well before Sully's time. This wood has the useful property of repelling insects; no sensible spider would spin a web in it. To make a similar roof, all you have to do is choose the best 100-year-old chestnut trees, use only the heartwood, soak it in water for several years to eliminate the sap, season it a while longer—say 80 years—and look out for a master carpenter who understands engineering stresses.

Hotel

Pont de Sologne (I), rue Porte de Sologne (tel. 38–36–26–34). 24 rooms, some with bath or shower. Closed late Dec. to mid-Jan. Good value for rooms and food.

Restaurant

L'Esplanade (M), pl. du Pilier (tel. 38–36–20–83). Closed Christmas to New Year's and Feb.; and Wed. except April through Sept. Across from the château. Cheery for drinks and à la carte specialties.

Fast Facts

Tourist Office: pl. Général-de-Gaulle (tel. 38–36–32–21).

Tours

Orientation

"No city in France exceeds it in beauty or delight," wrote John Evelyn, who spent 19 weeks here while on his Continental trip in 1644. He was pleased with the "long, straight, spacious, well-built and exceedingly clean streets," still a feature of the town. Henry James approved too, but there was less leisure for that particular hustling American on his Grand Tour: "Your business at Tours is to make excursions [which] divide themselves into the greater and the less. You may achieve most of the greater in a week or two; but a summer in Touraine would hold none too many days for the others."

James had to depend on trains in 1882, and Tours remains the ideal base on the Loire for those using public transportation. The French Railways booklet *Les Châteaux de la Loire en Train* gives details of services to Blois, Amboise, Beaugency, Langeais, Onzain, Chinon and Loches. Bicycles can be rented at those stations and left at any of the others; the brave can rent bikes in Tours itself, but Tours is a big, busy city. French Railways also organizes special château-visiting bus trips, including full- and half-day trips, and evening ones for *son et lumière*.

Drivers may prefer to base themselves in any of a dozen smaller places in the château-rich countryside within an hour of Tours. But don't be discouraged by the fact that Tours has recently mushroomed into a metropolis of a quarter of a million inhabitants, with a nasty modern sprawl of factories, skyscrapers and overpasses. The part of Tours that Evelyn and James knew is still as compact as a small town, and the A10 highway and the train will bring you almost into it. If you are planning a few days in Touraine, Tours deserves a visit right at the start.

The center of town is the big place du Maréchal Leclerc, more commonly called place de la Gare. Here is the train station, a fine *belle époque* structure with cast-iron curlicues cheerfully painted in primary colors; the bus station; the tourist office; and several hotels. Drivers can reach it by following the signs to "Centre Ville" or "Gare." For a sightseeing walk through the town, there is an all-day parking lot 200 yards away, off the wide boulevard next to the town hall, and another down rue Edouard Vaillant, which runs behind the station to the left. Drivers spending a night in the city should choose a hotel with a garage.

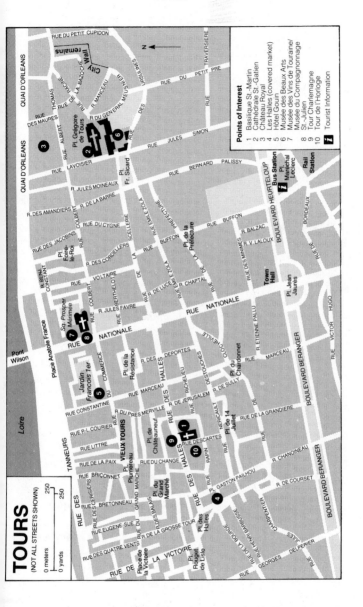

TOURS
(NOT ALL STREETS SHOWN)

0 meters   250
0 yards   250

Points of Interest

1 Basilique St-Martin
2 Cathédrale St-Gatien
3 Château Royal
4 Les Halles (covered market)
5 Hôtel Gouin
6 Musée des Beaux Arts
7 Musée des Vins de Touraine/
   Musée du Compagnonnage
8 St-Julien
9 Tour Charlemagne
10 Tour de l'Horloge
ℹ Tourist Information

History and Highlights

Tours was important in Roman times. Later, it had two famous early bishops, St. Martin and St. Gregory. St. Martin (316–397) did zealous missionary work in the region, and is always shown in pictures giving half his cloak to a beggar. Indian Summer is St. Martin's Summer in French, because, when his body was brought to Tours on a November day, flowers sprang into bloom. Gregory of Tours (538–594) was the author of the *History of the Franks,* highly readable and well translated into English. The short first part rushes from the creation of the world to Gregory's own time; the rest is a blow-by-blow account of daily events as seen from Tours. Later the Normans destroyed the abbey, which had been a center of learning under Alcuin of York.

From the 13th to 16th centuries Tours prospered, famous for fine buildings and elegant living, and for its luxury fabrics of silk and gold cloth. A decline set in with the Wars of Religion at the end of the 16th century. By the time the troubles were resolved under Henri IV, the court had left the Loire valley. The great complex of buildings around the Basilica of St. Martin had been sacked by Huguenots in 1562, and was finally destroyed at the Revolution; all that remains is the Tour de l'Horloge and the restored Tour de Charlemagne; the basilica built between 1887 and 1924 is by no means an architectural triumph.

By 1801 there were only 20,000 inhabitants in Tours. But the city was always an important center for communications, with the river, its bridges and—from 1846—a railway station. In 1870, in the Franco-Prussian War, the Germans bombarded and occupied it. Towards the end of World War I, it was the American army's administrative center. In 1940 the Germans bombarded it again, with greater effect. Much of the area around rue Nationale that Evelyn, Balzac and James knew was destroyed by fire, and in 1944 Allied bombers increased the damage while cutting the German lines of communication. Since the war the city has prospered enormously, damage has been repaired, and an intelligent rebuilding program has allowed the heart of the city to become once more a fine and interesting area for a lazy day's sightseeing and shopping.

Sights

Cathédrale St.-Gatien. Built between 1239 and 1484, the cathedral is a mixture of styles. Take binoculars if possible; the carvings on the capitals and stained glass, mercifully unharmed

Tours

during the last war, deserve their aid. Henry James is about right:

> . . . it is a very beautiful church of the second order of importance, with a charming mouse-colored complexion and a pair of fantastic towers . . . Its principal treasure perhaps is the charming little tomb of the two children (who died young) of Charles VIII and Anne of Brittany . . . The little boy and girl lie side by side on a slab of black marble, and a pair of small kneeling angels, both at their head and their feet, watch over them. Nothing could be more elegant than this monument.

Château Royal, quai d'Orléans. Containing **Historial** (wax museum) and **aquarium.** Open daily in winter 2–6; in summer 9–9; rest of year 9–12:30 and 2–7. Aquarium closed Mon. except in high season. English leaflets at both. Tels. (Historial) 47–61–46–04; (aquarium) 47–64–71–78.

What château? most people would have asked until recently. With one thing and another, it had almost totally disappeared. Some reconstruction has taken place, and a visit is recommended for those who like wax museums: the château houses the "Historial," figures of 165 personages in appropriate costumes —St.-Martin, Joan of Arc, Gambetta—whose deeds shaped the region. You can see this colorful display without a guide. The château also has a small aquarium.

Musée des Beaux Arts, 18 pl. François Sicard (tel. 47–05–68–73). Open daily, except Tues., 9–12:45 and 2–6. Located in a lovely 17th- and 18th-century building which used to be the archbishop's residence. It houses a number of treasures: Rubens, Rembrandt, Boucher, Degas, Alexander Calder—and Fritz the Elephant, stuffed in 1902, a left-over from a visit of Barnum's Circus. It also acts as the local gallery for traveling national art shows.

Musée des Vins de Touraine/Musée du Compagnonnage, 16 rue Nationale (tel. 47–61–07–93). Leaflets in English. Located in and around the cloisters and cellars of the church of St.-Julien, these two museums are not to be missed. The Guild Museum (*Musée du Compagnonnage*) celebrates the *compagnons,* craftsmen who learn their skill by making a tour of France, improving their technique before being admitted to the *compagnonnage,* a sort of trade union-*cum*-apprenticeship system. Here are the tools of many trades, and some amazing virtuoso work by candidates. Some of it is perverse: an Eiffel Tower in little pieces of slate, a château made of painted and varnished noodles, a chapel made of horseshoes. But all are fascinating, a tribute to the care, skill and painstaking devotion

to excellence that has been a feature of French life for centuries.
Vieux Tours. Crossing rue Nationale into rue du Commerce
and pl. Plumereau, you enter the oldest part of Tours, heavily
damaged in the war but now cleaned up and painstakingly
restored. This is a quaint area of picturesque little squares with
open-air cafes, eating places and antique shops. All trade to
some extent on their quaintness, but offer many temptations to
the idler nonetheless.

Hotels

Bordeaux (M), 3 pl. Maréchal Leclerc (tel. 47–05–40–32). 52
rooms, fully equipped.
Royal (M), 65 av. Grammont (tel. 47–64–71–78). 35 rooms
fully equipped. Garage; no restaurant.
L'Univers (M), 5 blvd. Heurteloup (tel. 47–05–37–12). 88
rooms, fully equipped. Garage. Restaurant closed Sat. A hundred years ago, Henry James found the staff here "so unnatural-
ly polite as at first to excite your suspicion that the hotel has
some hidden vice, so that the waiters and chambermaids are
trying to pacify in advance." They are still polite, and most of
the rooms look onto a quiet courtyard.
Akilène (I), 22 rue Grand Marché (tel. 47–61–46–04). 20
rooms with bath or shower. No restaurant. In a pedestrians-only
street near pl. Plumereau. Comfortable and simple. Convenient
to parking.
Armor (I), 26bis blvd. Heurteloup (tel. 47–05–24–37). 50
rooms with bath or shower. Central. No restaurant.

Restaurants

Charles Barrier (E), 101–103 av. de la Tranchee (tel. 47–54–20
–39). Closed Sun. evening and all day Mon. Having unfortu-
nately been obliged to retire for a brief period after a spot of
bother with the tax-man, M. Barrier's superb restaurant has
happily reopened its doors for business. It has instantly returned
to its former position as the best restaurant in Tours.
Les Tuffeaux (E), 19 rue Lavoisier (tel. 47–47–19–89). Closed
two weeks in Aug., three weeks in Jan.; Sun., Mon. The second
best restaurant in Tours. Michel Devaux does amazing things
with fish. His rabbit with prunes will at the first mouthful dissi-
pate prejudices against either or both of those items, and his
desserts are good.

Fast Facts

Tourist Office: pl. de la Gare (tel. 47–05–58–08). Open Mon. to Sat. 8:30–12:30 and 2–6 (1:30–9 in high season); Sun. and public holidays 10–12:30 and 3–6. English spoken. Books rooms, changes currency, hires guides, arranges tours by rail, copter and hot-air balloon. Coinoperated machine dispenses tourist literature after hours. "Audio guides"—cassettes for self-directed tours—may need advance reservation in high season.
Car Hire: *Avis,* 39bis blvd. Heurteloup (tel. 47–05–59–33); *Hertz,* 2 rue Fleming (tel. 47–61–02–54); *Europcar,* 76 rue Bernard Palissy (tel. 47–64–47–76).

Usse

Orientation

It is almost compulsory to call Ussé a fairy tale castle. Walt Disney studios must be well stocked with photographs of its white towers and pointed roofs, and tourist literature continually reminds you that *perhaps* Perrault had the place in mind when, in the 17th century, he wrote the story of Sleeping Beauty, *La Belle au Bois Dormant.*

Even if the charge is rather steep, even if there is a certain amount of good-natured fake—presumably aimed at children— about the Sleeping Beauty stuff, even if the leaflets in English hold the local record for misprints, you should not miss pretty Ussé, especially in light of the fact that it is in such lovely countryside and is so conveniently located, less than 15 km. (nine miles) from Azay-le-Rideau, Chinon and Langeais. The best approach to the castle is from Villandry, 20 km. (12 miles) away, following narrow, picturesque D16 along the Loire instead of the more usual D7.

The Château

Open daily mid-March through Sept., 9–12 and 2–6 or 7. Guided visit; leaflets in English. Allow 45 minutes. Tel. 47–95–54–05.

Ussé was started in the 15th century, but its 17th-century owners are responsible for most of it. A flamboyant mix of Gothic and Renaissance, it was built for fun. Its defenses were not for use, and almost nothing has ever happened here. There have been no gory political murders, and Catherine de Médicis never slept in the place. It was not even damaged in the Revolution; the owner prudently spent a few years in London and married there in 1797, as a tablet in the chapel shows. The Romantic writer Chateaubriand (1768–1848) gave the lady of the house the cedars that still adorn the grounds, and then jilted her. She wrote to him that she had stopped all the clocks in the house "so as never to hear struck the hours you will not come again." That is about all: happy the house that has no history!

The guided tour is worthwhile; the interior has good exhibits of furniture and tapestries, and a collection of 19th-century fashions displayed on models here and there. Visitors can go unguided up the spiral staircases to the *chemin de ronde*; there are pleasant views from the battlements of the river Indre snaking along. In the tower rooms, waxwork figures illustrate the Sleeping Beauty story. The little 16th-century chapel in the gardens is charming; there are agreeably sinister skull-and-crossbones carvings around the door, and inside is a fine ceramic Renaissance *bas relief* of the Virgin and Child by della Robbia.

Ussé

Valençay

Orientation

It would be sad to miss Valençay merely because it lies some distance south of the Loire, especially as a visit can be tied in so easily with tours of other châteaux. This town of 3,100 inhabitants is only 38 km. (23 miles) southeast of Montrichard via N76 and D956, and just 48 km. (29 miles) east of Loches. Loches and Valençay together are particularly suitable for a daytrip; the former offers medieval dungeons, the latter 19th-century sumptuousness, with vintage motor cars thrown in. Chenonceaux is a leisurely 55 km. (33 mile) drive away, along pretty, rural side roads. It is best, however, to arrive on the road from Blois, the same distance away; the imposing Renaissance-Classical château looms up above the road, and parking is easy to find on the wide main avenue—except on Tuesdays, when a market takes up the space.

History and Highlights

More a palace than a castle, Valençay was started in the 16th century, but most of the structure was built later. It was bought and sold several times. One of its owners was the Edinburgh economist John Law (1671–1729), whose brilliant schemes for reorganizing France's finances produced monster inflation and bankruptcy. He did not stay long.

The man who left his mark here was Talleyrand, alias the Limping Devil, the Sphinx, Charles-Maurice de Talleyrand-Péri-gord, Prince de Bénévent, the survival specialist who came out on top whatever the regime. Starting out as a very young but not very pious bishop under Louis XVI, he did quite well for himself in the Revolution and very well under Napoleon, survived Napoleon's fall and played a leading part in reshaping Europe at the Congress of Vienna after the Battle of Waterloo. Napoleon had earlier told Talleyrand, then Minister for Foreign Affairs, to buy himself a suitably noble country residence in which to weave his spells around visiting royalty and ambassadors; he bought Valençay in 1803. In these seductive surroundings he exercised his abilities—and enjoyed himself—until his death a quarter of a century later. A success story. The many rooms open to the public, with their luscious furniture and decoration, show how pleasant life can be if one has brains, money, taste, influence and no scruples whatsoever.

The Château

Open daily, mid-March to mid-Sept., 9–12 and 2–dusk; rest of year Sat., Sun. and public holidays only, same hours. Guided visit; leaflets in English. Some visits in English in July and Aug. Allow 45 minutes. Park and car museum same dates and times. Tel. 54–00–10–66.

Waits for guided visits can be long, but it's no problem to while away the time. The château entrance fronts onto a lovely French garden, with trimmed hedges, urns, statues, peacocks, ducks and flamingoes. Kangaroos, llamas and deer disport themselves in a broad park behind a wire fence.

In a big shed on the grounds is the **Musée de l'Automobile,** a collection of over 80 classic cars. With luck, you will find it in the charge of Mr. Roy Beard, an Englishman who came to Valençay in 1954, married a French girl and stayed. Among the exhibits is an 1898 Panhard, with two cylinders and six speeds (three in forward, three in reverse); a 1900 motor-bike for priests, with a little armchair and things for keeping cassocks out of the works; a charming Bedelia, a narrow two seater where the driver sits behind the passenger—it looks like an airplane without wings, with gleaming brass and a great belt drive—and other specimens offering near-Talleyrandian luxury.

Hotel

L'Espagne (E), 9 rue du Château (tel. 54–00–00–02). 11 rooms and 6 suites, fully equipped. Open mid-March to mid-Nov. Run for generations by the Fourré family, with a distinguished and expensive restaurant with outdoor seating.

Restaurant

Chêne Vert (I), tel. 54–00–06–54. Closed parts of June, Dec. and Jan.; Sun. and Sat. out of season. Decent food at reasonable prices. Outdoor tables.

Picnickers will find a good *charcuterie-rôtisserie* and a good *patisserie* next to the Espagne. There is a picnic area just outside of town off the road to Blois; fork left immediately towards Villentrois.

Valençay

Fast Facts

Tourist Office: In the parking lot, mid-June to mid-Sept. (tel. 54–00–04–42); rest of year at Hôtel de Ville (tel. 54–00–14–33).

Vendôme

Orientation

Vendôme's château is in ruins, and the town is not on most tourists' itineraries. It is nonetheless a charming place, just what a small French town should be. It lies 32 km. (19 miles) north of Blois, on the Loir (with no *e* and masculine—*la vallée du Loir,* as opposed to *la vallée de la Loire*).

There is modern development in a northern suburb, and much of the town was destroyed in 1940 and rebuilt rather unimaginatively. But the real center is still there, mercifully untouched and bypassed by through traffic. In it, the Loir divides into a multitude of channels. As you go from pedestrian street to pedestrian street, you keep crossing pretty little bridges, with old men fishing below. Predictably, leaflets from the Tourist Office call Vendôme "a flowery Venice." This is of course nonsense; one might as well call the other place an oversized, overpriced Vendôme. But a day's shopping and sightseeing here leaves an impression of gardens and streams, and of having everything near at hand.

A bus service connects Vendôme to Blois. Drivers coming from the Channel ports to the Loire (with an *e*) might consider breaking their journey here early in the afternoon, seeing the town and spending the night. Parking is in place de la Liberté, which doubles as the bus station. A pedestrian bridge over the river leads straight into rue de la Change.

Sights

Château. Open daily except Tues. March through June, 10–12 and 2–6; daily July and Aug., same hours. The gardens around the castle ruins give fine views of the town; a small admission charge ensures they are never crowded. They can be reached by climbing up a steep path; by car, leave the town through the impressive Porte St.-Georges, a 14th-century defensive gatehouse, and follow the signs to the château. Outside the gardens are wooded terraces with equally good views and a few tables and benches for picnics.

Musée. Open daily except Tues. and public holidays, 10–12 and 2–6. Leaflet in English. In the cloisters by the church, this is one of those charming provincial museums, a miscellaneous collection of tools of bygone trades, pictures and pleasant odds and ends, well worth a half-hour's ramble. The building is worth seeing too.

Place St.-Martin. This main square is dominated by a splendid 15th-century clock tower, which plays a traditional tune at the hour. Nearby is a statue of one of Vendôme's sons, Marshal Rochambeau, who helped the American revolutionaries and played a part in the British surrender at Yorktown in 1783. The statue is in fact a replica given to the town by the Society of Cincinnati in 1974; the earlier one had been melted down by the German non-ferrous metals squad in World War II. Rochambeau's château, which bears his name, is a few miles away and not open to the public. Britons may console themselves with the plaque on the clock tower, recording the gratitude of the Royal Flying Corps for hospitality in World War I.

La Trinité. Always open. Flamboyant and Gothic, built between the 12th and 15th centuries, the Abbey Church boasts an amazing detached clock tower, and a fine interior with good stained glass and wood carvings on the misericords. Misericords are little seats for monks to rest their bottoms on without actually sitting down during their endless daily offices; the carvings are on non-religious subjects only, given the nature of their use.

Hotels and Restaurants

Vendôme (M), 15 faubourg Chartrain (tel. 54–77–02–88). 35 rooms with bath or shower. Closed two weeks in Dec. Better value than comparable places along the Loire. Pleasant dining room with quietly efficient English-speaking service. Garage.

There are half a dozen other hotels in town, and a convenient **campsite** on the river.

In pl. St.-Martin, **Pierre Bouard** is famous for luxury pastries and chocolates, which can be sampled in the tea room. There is a fine market in the square on Fridays.

Fast Facts

Tourist Office: tour St.-Martin, rue Poterie (tel. 54–77–05–07). Postal address B.P. 34. Open daily.

Vendôme: Three misericords

Villaines-les-Rochers

Orientation

This village of 1,000 people is home to a wicker co-operative. It is not worth going far out of your way for, but a visit en route to Azay-le-Rideau, Saché or Villandry involves such a short detour that it can be heartily recommended. Look for signs to the Société Coopérative de Vannerie (*vannerie* is French for wickerwork).

The Wickerworks

Open daily most of the year, mornings and afternoons. Leaflet in English. Willows—or osiers, as they are more properly called—have long been cultivated near the Loire. The crop, cut in January, is treated, stored and worked in ideal conditions in workshops carved into the limestone cliffs. This beautiful skilled craft was on the point of dying out in 1849 when the parish priest convinced 65 small groups of basketweavers to form France's first agricultural producers' co-operative, centralizing orders, sales and dispatch. It is still flourishing. Its main output is baskets for bakeries and laundries, but the show-room has on display armchairs, sofas, cat-baskets, double beds and dress-maker's dummies. You can even buy them; this is one of those nice museums where you can take away the exhibits you like. Tourists with no room for such items in their cars will be tempted by elegant and inexpensive baby's rattles in traditional form—the noise is made by seven small pebbles, symbols of the seven deadly sins, rendered harmless by their virtuous cage.

There are picturesque troglodytic houses in the village, where basket-weavers live and work.

Villandry

Orientation

Just 20 km. (12 miles) southwest of Tours and 10 km. (six miles) northeast of Azay-le-Rideau on D7, Villandry retains its reputation for charm and uniqueness in an area where there's no shortage of châteaux. For the past 60 years, ordinary visitors and specialists alike have flocked to Villandry for its unusual gardens.

The Château and Gardens

Château: open daily 9–5, 6 or 6:30, depending on season. Guided visit; leaflets in English. Gardens: open daily 8:30 or 9–6:30 or 8, depending on season. Wander freely. Tel. 47–50–02–07.

Jean Breton, secretary of state to François I, began the châ-

Villandry: The gardens

teau in the 16th century. But the history of the château in the days of François, Napoleon and the others pales in comparison to its rejuvenation at the hands of Dr. Joachim Carvallo, a Spaniard born in 1869. Carvallo was doing medical research in Paris when he fell in love with fellow-student Ann Coleman, a steel heiress from Philadelphia, and married her. The Carvallos bought the château in 1906, when it was run down and on the point of demolition. Ruthlessly eliminating recent accretions, they restored the building to its ancient grandeur and furnished its rooms. More importantly, they replanted the gardens, creating in rigorously geometrical 16th-century fashion all the close-trimmed swirling and zig-zagging hedges that enclosed the flower-beds, vegetable plots and gravel walks of an aristocratic *jardin à la française*. The current owner is Joachim and Ann Carvallo's grandson, who is barely able to keep the gardens going thanks to a small state subsidy and admission charges.

Long avenues of precisely pruned lime trees—there are 1,500 of them, with hardly a leaf out of place—lead to a terrace at the back. Behind is an ornamental lake flowing down to a moat full of swans. Farther behind is back-stage, where as many as 10,-000 seedlings wait in pots under glass, behind mounds of well-rotted horse manure, for the moment when they will be planted out at points determined to the nearest millimeter. To the right is another terrace, which looks down on the château and on the multicolored cabbages parading in some of the complicated enclosures formed by 19 km. (12 miles) of close-clipped low hedges; other sights include the flowers, of course, and the drilled pear tress, and the "aromatic and medicinal garden," with each plant neatly labeled in three languages.

This precision disconcerts some people. Villandry deviates completely from the cunningly "natural" rules Capability Brown laid down for 18th-century English gentlemen's parks; here, nature is as unnatural as a grand opera. But even those whose tastes are staunchly romantic rather than classical are unlikely to regret seeing this unique reconstruction of the past.

The château's interior is beguiling as well. Joachim Carvallo decorated it with many treasures from his native Spain, including a remarkable painted and gilded ceiling from Toledo. There is a good collection of Spanish pictures, including a couple of Goyas and one work from the School of Velásquez.

Because the château and gardens do not close at mid-day, you can often have them all to yourself while the French eat lunch. There is an excellent and lavishly-illustrated leaflet on sale, in better English than is often the case—not surprisingly, as it is a reprint of a long article in *House and Garden,* aptly entitled "The Geometry of Pleasure."

Hotel

Le Cheval Rouge (M), tel. 47–50–02–07. 20 rooms with bath or shower. Open March through Oct. Closed Mon. except May through Aug. Restaurant is popular with discerning locals; excellent dishes and Loire wine list. Don't confuse it with the café of the same name outside the château entrance.

ENGLISH-FRENCH TOURIST VOCABULARY

Basics

yes	oui
no	non
please	s'il vous plaît
thank you	merci
thank you very much	merci bien
excuse me, sorry	pardon
I'm sorry	je suis désolé(e), je regrette
good morning, good afternoon, hello	bonjour
good evening	bonsoir
good night	bonne nuit
goodbye	au revoir

Numbers

1	un	16	seize
2	deux	17	dix-sept
3	trois	18	dix-huit
4	quatre	19	dix-neuf
5	cinq	20	vingt
6	six	21	vingt-et-un
7	sept	30	trente
8	huit	40	quarante
9	neuf	50	cinquante
10	dix	60	soixante
11	onze	70	soixante-dix
12	douze	80	quatre-vingts
13	treize	90	quatre-vingt-dix
14	quatorze	100	cent
15	quinze	1000	mille

Days of the Week

Sunday	dimanche
Monday	lundi
Tuesday	mardi
Wednesday	mercredi
Thursday	jeudi
Friday	vendredi
Saturday	samedi

Months

January	janvier
February	février
March	mars
April	avril
May	mai
June	juin
July	juillet
August	août
September	septembre
October	octobre
November	novembre
December	décembre

Useful Questions and Answers

Do you speak English?	Parlez-vous anglais?
What time is it?	Quelle heure est-il?
Is this seat free?	Est-ce que cette place est libre?
How much does it cost?	Quel est le prix, s'il vous plaît?
Would you please direct me to . . . ?	Quel est le chemin pour . . . ?
Where is the station, museum . . .?	Pour aller à la gare, au musée, s'il vous plaît?
I am American, British	Je suis américain(e), anglais(e)
It's very kind of you	Vous êtes bien aimable
I don't understand	Je ne comprends pas
I don't know	Je ne sais pas
Please speak more slowly	Parlez plus lentement, s'il vous plaît
Please sit down	Asseyez-vous, je vous en prie

Everyday Needs

cigar, cigarettes	cigare, cigarette
matches	allumettes
dictionary	dictionnaire
key	clef
razor blades	lames de rasoir
shaving cream	mousse à barbe
soap	savon
city plan	plan de la ville
road map	carte routière
country map	carte géographique
newspaper	journal
magazine	magazine, revue
telephone	téléphone
telegram	télégramme
envelopes	enveloppes
writing paper	papier à lettres

airmail writing paper	papier avion
post card	carte postale
stamp	timbre

Services and Stores

bakery	boulangerie
bookshop	librairie
butcher's	boucherie
delicatessen	charcuterie
dry cleaner's	pressing
grocery	épicerie
hairdresser, barber	coiffeur
laundry	blanchisserie
laundromat	laverie automatique
shoemaker	cordonnerie
stationery store	papeterie
supermarket	supermarché

Emergencies

ill, sick	malade
I am ill	Je suis malade
My wife/husband/child is ill	Mon épouse/mon mari/mon enfant est malade
doctor	médecin
nurse	infirmier/infirmière
prescription	ordonnance
pharmacist/chemist	pharmacien
Please fetch/call a doctor	Veuillez chercher/appeler un médecin
accident	accident
road accident	accident de la route
Where is the nearest hospital?	Veuillez m'indiquer l'hôpital/ la clinique le/la plus proche
dentist	dentiste
X-ray	radio

Pharmacist's

pain-killer	analgèsique
gauze pads	carré de gaze
bandage	pansement
bandaid	sparadrap
scissors	ciseaux
hot-water bottle	bouillotte
sanitary pads	serviettes hygiéniques
ointment for bites/stings	pommade pour les pîqures
coughdrops	pastilles pour la gorge
cough mixture	sirop anti-tussif
laxative	laxatif

Traveling

plane	avion
hovercraft	aéroglisseur
train	train
boat	bateau/ferry
taxi	taxi
car	voiture
seat	place
reservation	réservation
smoking/non-smoking compartment	salle fumeurs/non-fumeurs
rail station	gare
subway station	station
airport	aéroport
harbor	port
town terminal	terminus en ville
shuttle bus/train	navette
sleeper	wagon-lit
couchette	couchette
porter	porteur
baggage/luggage	bagages
baggage trolley	chariot
single ticket	aller
return ticket	aller-retour
first class	première classe
second class	deuxième/seconde classe

When does the train leave?	Le train part à quelle heure?
What time does the train arrive at . . . ?	Le train arrive à . . . à quelle heure?
When does the first/last train leave?	A quelle heure part le premier/le dernier train?

Hotels

room	chambre
bed	lit
bathroom	salle de bains
bathtub	baignoire
shower	douche
toilet, lavatory	toilettes, WC (*pron.* vay-say)
toilet paper	papier hygiénique
pillow	oreiller
blanket	couverture
chambermaid	femme de chambre
breakfast	petit déjeuner
lunch	déjeuner
dinner	dîner

Do you have a single/double /twin-bedded room?	Auriez-vous une chambre single/à grand lit/à deux lits?
I'd like a quiet room	Je voudrais une chambre calme
I'd like some pillows	Je voudrais des oreillers
What time is breakfast?	On sert le petit déjeuner de quelle heure à quelle heure?
Come in!	Entrez!
Are there any messages for me?	Auriez-vous un message pour moi?
Would you please call me a taxi?	J'aurais aimé un taxi, s'il vous plaît
Please take our bags to our room	Veuillez emmener nos bagages à la chambre

Restaurants

menu	carte
fixed-price menu	menu
wine list	carte des vins
waiter	serveur
Waiter!	Monsieur, s'il vous plaît
bill/check	addition/note

On The Menu

Starters

crudités	raw vegetables
escargot	snail
hors d'oeuvres variés	mixed hors d'oeuvre
melon	melon
pâté	finely chopped and pressed meat, baked
potage	soup
terrine	a rougher version of pâté

Meats (Viande)

agneau	lamb	jambon	ham
biftec	steak	lapin	rabbit
boeuf	beef	lard	bacon
brochette	kebab	mouton	mutton
charcuterie	pork cold cuts	porc	pork
châteaubriand	fillet steak	rosbif	roastbeef
côte, côtelette	chop	saucisse	sausage
entrecôte	rib steak	saucisson	salami
gigot d'agneau	leg of lamb	veau	veal

Poultry (Volaille) and Game (Gibier)

caille	quail	pintade/	guinea hen/
canard	duck	pintadeau	fowl
caneton	duckling	poule	boiling fowl
coq	young cockerel	poulet	chicken
faisan	pheasant	poussin	spring
marcassin	wild boar		chicken
oie	goose		
perdreau	partridge		

Variety Meats, Offal (Abats)

cervelle	brains	ris	kidney
foie	liver	rognon	sweetbreads
langue	tongue	tripes	tripe

Fish (Poisson)

anguille	eel	merlan	whiting
cabillaud	cod	perche	perch
daurade	sea bream	saumon	salmon
lotte	monkfish	truite	trout
loup de mer	sea bass	truite saumonée	salmon trout
maquereau	mackerel		

Shellfish (Coquillages, Crustacés)

bouquet	prawn	langouste	spiny rock
crevettes	shrimp		lobster,
ecrevisses	crawfish		crayfish
escargots	snails	langoustines	scampi
fruits de mer	mixed shellfish	moules	mussels
cuisses de gren-		oursin	sea urchin
ouilles	frogs' legs	palourdes	cockles
homard	lobster	praires	clams
huîtres	oysters		

Vegetables (Légumes)

artichaut	globe artichoke	haricot vert	French bean
asperge	asparagus	lentille	lentils
aubergine	eggplant	navet	turnip
carotte	carrot	oignon	onion
champignon	mushroom	oseille	sorrel
chou	cabbage	pomme de terre	potato
choucroute	sauerkraut	petit pois	pea
choufleur	cauliflower	poireau	leek
courgette	zucchini	poivron	green/red
~~esson~~	watercress		pepper
~~·ive~~	chicory	riz	rice
~~·ds~~	spinach	salade	lettuce

fève	broad bean	tomate	tomato
flageolet	kidney bean (green)	topinambour	Jerusalem
haricot blanc	white haricot bean		artichoke

Fruit

ananas	pineapple	mûr	blackberry
cassis	blackcurrant		(bramble)
cerise	cherry	myrtille	bilberry
citron	lemon	orange	orange
fraise	strawberry	pamplemousse	grapefruit
fraise des bois	wild strawberry	pastèque	watermelon
		pêche	peach
framboise	raspberry	poire	pear
groseille	redcurrant	pomme	apple
groseille à maquereau	gooseberry	prune	plum
		pruneau	prune

Desserts

beignet	fritter	chocolat	mousse
crème caramel	caramel custard	salade des fruits	fruit salad
gâteau	cake	sorbet	water ice
glace	ice cream	tarte	pie/tart/flan
mousse au	chocolate		

Sauces and Styles

aïoli	garlic mayonnaise	indienne	curried
béarnaise	sauce made from egg, butter and herbs	niçoise	prepared with oil, garlic, tomatoes and onions
bien cuit	well done		
bordelaise	prepared with red claret, garlic, onions and mushrooms	poêlé	fried, sautéed
		à point	medium (steak)
à la broche	spit-roasted	rose	lightly roasted
bleu	very rare (steak)		
Chantilly	with whipped cream	rôti	roast
		saignant	rare (steak)
croustade	baked pastry shell	vinaigrette	with oil and vinegar dressing
flambé	flamed with warmed brandy		
fricassé	braised, fried		
fumé	smoked		
au gratin	browned under grill (perhaps with grated cheese)		